Helion & Company Limited
Unit 8 Amherst Business Centre
Budbrooke Road
Warwick
CV34 5WE
England
Tel. 01926 499 619
Email: info@helion.co.uk
Website: www.helion.co.uk
Twitter: @helionbooks
Visit our blog http://blog.helion.co.uk/

Designed and typeset by Farr out Publications, Wokingham, Berkshire
Cover design Paul Hewitt, Battlefield Design (www.battlefield-design.co.uk)

Cover photo: A Yak-25M interceptor of the 147th Guards Interceptor Aviation Regiment based at Monchegorsk AB, on the Kola Peninsula, in 1962. (via EasternOrbat.com)

Cover artwork: A MiG-17F of the 117th Interceptor Aviation Regiment, PVO, piloted by Senior Lieutenant Kucheryaev during the intercept of C-130A-II serial number 60-258 in the skies over Soviet Armenia on 2 September 1958. (Artwork by Tom Cooper)

ISBN 978-1-915070-71-5

British Library Cataloguing-in-Publication Data
A catalogue record for this book is available from the British Library

We always welcome receiving book proposals from prospective authors.

CONTENTS

MAP OF EUROPE 1945–1992

Note: In order to simplify the use of this book, all names, locations and geographic designations are as provided in *The Times World Atlas*, or other traditionally accepted major sources of reference, as of the time of described events.

ABBREVIATIONS

AA	Anti-aircraft
AAM	Air-to-air missile
AB	Air Base
AD	Air Defence
AFB	Air Force Base
ASCC	Air Standardisation Coordinating Committee
BuNo	Bureau Number, a designation for aircraft assigned by the US Navy Bureau of Aeronautics
CIA	Central Intelligence Agency
COMINT	Communications Intelligence
DC	Douglas Commercial (transport and passenger aircraft made by the US aerospace manufacturer Douglas)
ELINT	Electronic Intelligence
FRA	*Försvarets Radioanstalt* – Defence Radio Establishment (a Swedish government agency under the country's Ministry of Defence which is amongst others responsible for signals intelligence)
GCI	Ground Control Intercept
GIAP	*Gvardeyskiy Istrebitelniy Aviatsionniy Polk* – Guards Fighter Aviation Regiment (Soviet tactical fighter unit)
IAP	*Istrebitelniy Aviatsionniy Polk* – Fighter Aviation Regiment (Soviet tactical fighter unit)
IFF	Identification Friend or Foe
Il	Ilyushin (the design bureau headed by Sergey Ilyushin)
Ju	Junkers (a German aircraft designer and manufacturer)
KB-1	*Konstruktorskoye Byuro-1* – Construction Bureau no. 1, formerly SB-1
KGB	*Komitet Gosudarstvennoy Bezopasnosti* – State Security Committee (the main security agency of the Soviet Union)
La	Lavochkin (the design bureau headed by Semyon Lavochkin), also known as NPO Lavochkin or OKB-301
LEMZ	*Lianozovskiy Elektromekhanicheskiy Zavod* – Lianozovsky Electromechanical Plant – a Soviet manufacturer of radars and electronics
MiG	Mikoyan i Gurevich – the design bureau led by Artyom Ivanovich Mikoyan and Mikhail Iosifovich Gurevich, also known as OKB-155 or MMZ 'Zenit')
MTAP	*Minno-Torpednyy Aviatsionnyy Polk* – Mine-Torpedo Aviation Regiment (a Soviet naval aviation tactical unit tasked with aerial delivery of sea mines and surface strike by means of torpedoes)
NATO	North Atlantic Treaty Organization
NNIIRT	*Nizhegorodskiy Nauchno-Issledovatelskiy Institut Radiotekhniki* – the Nizhny Novgorod Research Institute of Radio Engineering – one of the main Soviet developers and manufacturers of radars and associated electronics
PVO	*Protivovozdushnaya Oborona* – literally air defence but frequently used to denote the Air Defence Troops
PRC	People's Republic of China, the mainland Chinese communist state
RAF	Royal Air Force (of the United Kingdom)
ROCAF	Republic of China Air Force
SAC	Strategic Air Command
SAM	Surface-to-air missile
SB-1	*Spetsialnoye Byuro-1* – Special Bureau-1 – the design bureau entrusted with developing the S-25 Berkut SAM system (ASCC/NATO-codename 'SA-1 Guild'), subsequently renamed KB-1
SENSINT	Sensitive Intelligence
SIGINT	Signals Intelligence
Su	Sukhoi (the design bureau led by Pavel Ossipovich Sukhoi, also known as OKB-51)
Tu	Tupolev (the design bureau headed by Andrei Tupolev, also known as OKB-156)
US/USA	United States/of America
USAF	United States Air Force
USN	United States Navy
USRJC	US–Russia Joint Commission on POWs/MIAs
USSR	Union of Soviet Socialist Republics
VNIIRT	*Vserossiyskiy Nauchno-Issledovatelskiy Institut Radiotekhniki* – the All-Russian Research Institute of Radio Engineering, one of the main Soviet developers and manufacturers of radars and associated electronics
VNOS	*Vozdushnoye Nablyudeniye, Opoveshcheniye y Svyaz* – Aerial Surveillance, warning and communications – early Soviet air warning network mostly relaying on visual observation posts
Yak	Yakovlev (the design bureau led by Alexander Yakovlev, also known as OKB-115 or MMZ 'Skorost')

A FEW INTRODUCTORY NOTES

When selecting the title for this project, we have considered several versions. 'Defending Homeland' did not sound 'Russian enough' to the authors and editors, and could be misunderstood. Therefore, we opted for a mix of English and Russian. 'Rodina' is Russian for 'homeland', 'motherland', 'native land', or 'birthplace'. In the Russian language, the accusative case is an indirect case and answers the questions like whom, what, or where. Its application results in different noun endings, depending on whether they have animacy, and whether they are masculine or feminine. Feminine accusative case ending for Rodina is 'u'. Considering this, we have opted for 'Defending Rodinu'.

Fighter aircraft (or 'manned interceptors') and ground-based air defences were, in the period which is the subject of this volume, deployed not only on the territory of the Union of Soviet Socialist Republics (USSR, colloquially the 'Soviet Union'): Soviet fighter aircraft were deployed on the territory of a number of other states. In particular, a large contingent of Soviet fighter aircraft, pilots and other personnel was stationed in the People's Republic of China (PRC). There, they fought in the Chinese and Korean skies. At the same time, numerous aerial engagements took place, some of which were borderline in nature both literally as well as figuratively speaking. It can be argued that some of the incidents related herein were in fact part of the Korean War, yet it also stands to reason that they were Cold War incidents resulting from the violation of Soviet airspace (whether factual or merely asserted). The author has taken the liberty to use his judgment and discretion regarding the inclusion or exclusion of such incidents, going by the general rule that should an incident have taken place in Soviet airspace, even if only just over the borderline or in its immediate vicinity, it is to be covered; otherwise it will be omitted. There are of course exceptions and caveats, in particular when dealing with events which unfolded over the sea. Similarly, the temporal dimension may also raise questions, since during the Second World War, Soviet and US aircraft clashed on a number of occasions and one can with some justification view such incidents as a herald of things to come during the Cold War. However, even if certain events during the Second World War foreshadowed the subsequent Cold War, both conflicts should be clearly separated. Otherwise, by tying one past event continually to another, it would be unavoidable to endlessly go back into history. For this reason, any US-Soviet incidents which took place before the capitulation of Germany in Europe and Japan in the Far East are completely excluded. It is the author's opinion that even if not perfect, the choices made (the reasoning for which was outlined above) regarding the subject at hand do not abuse general standards of logic and common sense.

The bold and – no doubt provocative – reconnaissance operations flown by the US and allies between 1945 and 1992, and Soviet efforts to counter such, constituted an important part of how the Cold War was fought. For it was an armed conflict and it was fought, even if usually not as intensively as some all-out conflicts before, during, or since. A full-scale confrontation always loomed in the background and should it have ever come to pass (which as we know in the end it did not), to a large extent it would have had to play itself out in the air, if for no other reason than because in the early to mid-Cold War period, bomber aircraft armed with nuclear weapons became the primary means of strategic attack. Thus, in order to have an understanding of the rivalry between the USA and the USSR, both within the realms of aviation and as a whole, a description of Soviet air defences and a narrative of their operations seems indispensable. For these reasons, the present volume aims to provide an account, one which will reasonably balance the need to remain succinct while also being detailed, of how post-war Soviet air defences were developed and how they countered US and other Western aerial reconnaissance operations, while also providing the overall historical as well as political context. However, exhaustive technical descriptions of aircraft, weapons, equipment and so on have been dispensed with (general ones being provided instead) for such can be found in numerous monographs which in turn usually describe operational and combat deployment of a given type only in a most cursory manner – in contrast, that (and other information) is what the reader is provided with herein.

ACKNOWLEDGEMENTS

It is impossible for a project such as this to materialise in the tangible form of a book without many helping hands lending their support, advice, and practical assistance. Thus, the author finds it indispensable to express his most sincere gratitude to Dymitry Zubkov and Tom Cooper as well as many others, thanks to whom this volume came into being.

INTRODUCTION

Once the Second World War was victoriously concluded, Soviet-American amity ended. In no time, the USA (the West by extension) was confronted by the USSR, a state which was secretive and militarised as well as being a state which adhered to an ideology both expansionist and totalitarian. Avoiding a surprise attack and learning what the Soviets were otherwise concocting was thus of utmost importance. Considering those circumstances, the aerial reconnaissance of the USSR seemed an imperative dictated by sheer self-preservation. Yet it would be a gross oversimplification and distortion to claim that doing so served only defensive purposes. Plans for a nuclear war against the Soviet Union were made (even if never implemented) and they required data about potential targets as well as defences, with aerial reconnaissance again being the best (and sometimes only) way to gather it.

Meanwhile, the Soviets were also dealing with the Second World War's aftermath and the resulting circumstances. Large areas in the European part of the USSR were devastated, though reconstruction and the building of completely new industrial and military facilities was in full swing. In order to target them, the potential enemy had to have accurate data on their locations and such acquisition of data obviously had to be prevented. The prospect of a US nuclear attack was a realistic possibility, especially when the Americans enjoyed a nuclear monopoly, and there was no reason to make it easier for them. Even after the USSR developed nuclear weapons of its own, it still lagged behind considerably in strategic weapons delivery capabilities. This weakness could also be seen as an invitation for a debilitating American nuclear strike and thus it was logical to keep the Americans guessing about the actual Soviet potential to retaliate. All that in turn meant that American and other Western reconnaissance aircraft had to be vigorously combated. If the Americans needed to 'remember Pearl Harbor', the Soviets remembered how Luftwaffe reconnaissance aircraft were allowed to roam almost unhindered on the eve of Operation Barbarossa.

Faced with the threats and challenges outlined above, it is not surprising that the Soviets strived to organise a structurally efficient air defence force and to equip it with all the technical means necessary to fulfil its mission. This resulted in the vigorous development of air surveillance radars and automated control systems, plus successive models of jet-powered fighter aircraft each with improved performance – in particular, with ever-increasing speed and operational altitude as well as on-board radars and guided air-to-air missiles. Additionally, conventional anti-aircraft artillery followed by guided surface-to-air missiles were also fielded in considerable numbers. How this impressive arsenal was forged and how it went into action when circumstances called for it is laid out below.

1
BIRTH OF THE POST-WAR SOVIET AIR DEFENCE FORCE

During the Second World War – or the 'Great Patriotic War', as it became known in the USSR – the German Luftwaffe was, as a general rule (a few exceptions notwithstanding), not able to carry out offensive aerial operations beyond a few hundred kilometres from the frontline, and was not able to mount a truly strategic bombing offensive against vitally important targets deep within Soviet territory. However, the war had barely ended when the USSR found itself at odds with its erstwhile Western allies. The threat posed by Western, and in particular American, airpower was of a different nature, as was amply demonstrated during the Second World War: massive, sustained and very destructive strategic air campaigns were conducted against the Axis powers, Germany and Japan in particular. Moreover, the dropping of nuclear bombs on Hiroshima and Nagasaki in August 1945 showed that the US could bring to bear previously almost unimaginable devastation upon its enemies. Therefore, since a confrontation with the West was looming, in 1946 the leadership of the USSR decided to deploy air defences throughout the entire territory of the country.[1]

Both the prospect of an all-out war as well as the need to fend off peacetime intruders called for an effective organisation of air defences. For that purpose, in 1948 the USSR's territory was broadly divided into two categories: border areas and internal areas. The former were designated PPVO (*Prigranichnyye Polosy Vozdushnoy Oborony*, translating as Border (frontier) Air Defence Belts (zones)) in which the VOPL (*Vozdushnuyu Oboronu Prigranichnoy Linii*, Air Defence of the Border Line) would be organised.[2] Meanwhile, the Soviet interior was to be divided into Air Defence Districts which were subsequently reorganised into AD Regions, known as PVO TS (*Protivovozdushnaya Oborona Territorii Strany*, Air Defence of the Country's Territory). The responsibility of actually conducting air defence operations was shared between Military Districts, Fleets of the Soviet Navy and Air Defence Districts. There were several organisational changes in the first half of the 1950s as to who would be responsible for what and where, as well as some commands disbanding while new ones were set up, but none of those rearrangements were ever satisfactory.

The Korean War reconfirmed the menace that Western airpower constituted and even though a 'hot war' with direct attacks against USSR territory (aside from a single incident described separately) did not break out, the Cold War was meanwhile in full swing with numerous incursions into Soviet airspace by foreign reconnaissance aircraft on a semi-regular basis. In particular, deep penetrations of Soviet airspace – especially a whole series of such events in 1954 which will be described in Chapter Nine – demonstrated beyond any doubt that air defences were organisationally inefficient and lacked the means to be up to the task. A different approach was clearly needed and on 27 May 1954, both the Central Committee of the Communist Party and the Council of Ministers of the USSR promulgated a resolution addressing the problem which, among others, decreed that the country's air defences had to be reorganised and re-equipped.[3] This was followed by an appropriate order of the Ministry of Defence, dated 14 June 1954.[4]

Consequently, the air defence (p*rotivovozdushnaya oborona*) was to be restructured and elevated to the status of a separate branch of the Soviet Armed Forces. Thus the *Voyska Protivovozdushnoy Oborony* (V-PVO) were to be composed of three principal elements: *Istrebitelnaya Aviatsiya* (fighter aviation), *Zenitnyye Raketnyye Voyska* (anti-aircraft rockets, that is, missile troops) and *Radiotekhnicheskiye Voyska* (radio-technical, that is, radar troops). The guiding idea was that the V-PVO would be responsible for the air defence of the entire territory of the Soviet Union, having all the assets needed for the task, and would coordinate actions between them. In addition, this would also result in a clear delimitation of responsibilities: ground force units and fleets would be left only with organic AD capabilities for their own protection from air attack without responsibility for that of the country's territory; similarly, fighter units of the *Voyenno-Vozdushnyye Sily* (VVS, Soviet Air Force) were to have a tactical role separate from that of the PVO fighter aviation's sole mission of defending Soviet airspace.

As a result, by the end of the 1950s and the beginning of the 1960s, the PVO would gain the following basic structure (for a map of the following organisation, see the colour section):

PVO Headquarters Moscow

- Moscow Air Defence District (Moscow)
- Baku Air Defence District (Baku)
- 2 Separate (Independent) Air Defence Army (Minsk)
- 4 Separate (Independent) Air Defence Army (Sverdlovsk, modern Yekaterinburg)
- 6 Separate (Independent) Air Defence Army (Leningrad, modern St. Petersburg)
- 8 Separate (Independent) Air Defence Army (Kiev)
- 10 Separate (Independent) Air Defence Army (Arkhangelsk)
- 11 Separate (Independent) Air Defence Army (Khabarovsk)
- 12 Separate (Independent) Air Defence Army (Tashkent)
- 14 Separate (Independent) Air Defence Army (Novosibirsk)

Generally, an AD district or army would have a number of subordinate AD corps which, in turn, were composed of AD divisions and other units of a lower order, though in some cases AD divisions were under the direct control of an AD district or army. A notable exception was the Moscow AD District which had in its structure an AD army solely tasked with operating the S-25 SAM rings around the Soviet capital (see below for details). While over time some units were disbanded, others raised in the basic structure outlined above remained in place for the next 20 years until the 1980s.

Soviet Ground-Based Airspace Surveillance and Interception Control

Any organisation, no matter how theoretically efficient it should be, is only as capable as facilitated by the means at its disposal. In order to provide an effective air defence, airborne threats have to be detected in the first place. The Soviet ground-based early warning network was called the VNOS (*Vozdushnoye Nablyudeniye, Opoveshcheniye y Svyaz,* Aerial Surveillance, Warning and Communications). For the purpose of detecting aerial threats, the Soviets heavily relied on visual observation posts and their reports. However, not only were such posts not sufficient in numbers and density but also their reporting as well as the processing of said reports, and the coordination between air defence assets once such reports were received, left much to be desired.[5] Visual observation posts aside, the Soviets also had radars: the first RUS-1 radar sets entered service in 1940, soon followed by the RUS-2 and additional models. Domestic development efforts were greatly aided by the deliveries of Western radars during the Second World War as well as by captured German technology acquired when the Soviets overran large parts of Germany by the war's end.[6] The ever-wider use of radars for early warning was slowly changing the character of the VNOS which would eventually be disbanded on 15 December 1951[7] with its assets taken over by the then-established *Radiotekhnicheskiye Voyska* ('radio-technical', that is, radar troops) which in turn were subsequently integrated into the PVO (see above). Yet the radar troops also suffered from basically the same weaknesses as the VNOS, which first and foremost stemmed from the fact that the number of radars in their inventory was too small. It is therefore not surprising that Western aircraft utilising gaps in radar coverage were sometimes able to penetrate deep over Soviet territory to carry out reconnaissance missions and to drop agents, particularly in the early stages of the Cold War. However, such 'happy times' were not to last forever as Soviet defence establishments were striving to develop a number of radars with a variety of models each best suited for a particular task.

Concerning the aforementioned radars, one of the main developers and suppliers of radars in the Soviet Union was the Nizhny Novgorod-based NNIIRT.[8] Among its early creations was the P-3 (ASCC/NATO-codename 'Dumbo') air surveillance radar which, figuratively speaking, connected late-war with early post-war radar development. During the 1950s a whole range of air surveillance radars was introduced into service: the P-8, P-12 and P-15 (ASCC/NATO-codenames 'Knife Rest', 'Spoon Rest' and 'Flat Face') with this line-up being far from exhaustive. Of note is that towards the end of the decade, the P-14 (ASCC/NATO-codename 'Tall King') long-range detection and tracking radar entered service. An important part in setting up effective air defences was also played by early warning/surveillance and ground control radars developed by VNIIRT: the P-20 and P-30 (ASCC/NATO-codenames 'Bar Lock' and 'Big Mesh') as well as the P-35 (also using the ASCC/NATO-codename 'Bar Lock'), the latter manufactured by LEMZ. The growing number of radars allowed the establishment of an ever-tighter radar network which in the 1950s at the very least facilitated the detection and tracking of foreign aircraft along large sections of the USSR's borders and in the internal areas which were considered important.[9]

A P-8 air surveillance radar (ASCC/NATO-codename 'Knife Rest'): one of first systems of this kind in Soviet service. (Soviet Ministry of Defence)

The P-12M air surveillance radar (ASCC/NATO-codename 'Spoon Rest'). (Soviet Ministry of Defence)

The P-20 air surveillance/early warning and ground control radar (ASCC/NATO-codename 'Bar Lock'). (Soviet Ministry of Defence)

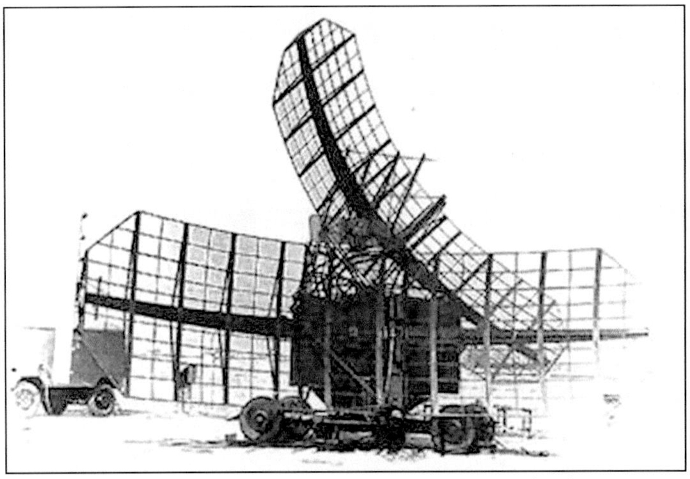

A P-30 air surveillance/early warning and ground control radar (ASCC/NATO-codename 'Big Mesh'). (Soviet Ministry of Defence)

Having radars and being able to detect threats was an obvious necessity but was not an end in itself. What was called for was the capability to effectively process the information provided by transforming it into data which could be swiftly and reliably relayed so as to facilitate an interception. For this to be so, a systemic approach was necessary, linking radars and other assets into one functional entity or a *kompleks* (complex) as the Soviets preferred to call it. Efforts to develop such were in progress throughout the 1950s. Its practical workability was proven during tests which could be described as proof-of-concept trials conducted in the Kursk region in September 1956.[10] The ground-based system received the designation *Vozdukh*: it linked radars feeding information they provided to *Kaskad* analogue computers that processed them into guidance data for interception which was in turn relayed via the *Lazur* radio command link to fighter aircraft so as to optimally position them for engaging a target with their missile armament. Work on such aircraft and armaments, as will be separately described below, was meanwhile going on, resulting in the first fighter type equipped to work with it: the Su-9 (ASCC/NATO-codename 'Fishpot') which together with its weapons fit of RS-2US (ASCC/NATO-codename 'AA-1 Alkali') guided air-to-air missiles made up a *kompleks perekhvata,* an interception complex or system. When both were ready, operational trials of the ground-based system and its interaction with the airborne component started in January 1960 and once they were successfully concluded its deployment began the very same year.[11] For its time, the *Vozdukh* system was highly automated and capable as it was theoretically able to provide interception data for targets at a distance of up to 1,200 kilometres operating at altitudes between 250 metres and 31,750 metres which was higher than any weapon available to the Soviets at that time could reach. Obviously, the range, altitude and so on of the target which could be detected, tracked and engaged depended on numerous factors and could in practice differ considerably case-by-case. Subsequently, the system was continuously developed, gaining capabilities and when new fighter-interceptor types entered service they too were fitted to work with it.

2

SOVIET GROUND-BASED AIR DEFENCE WEAPONS OF THE EARLY COLD WAR PERIOD

The Soviet military has historically attached considerable importance to the development and fielding of ground-based air defence weaponry. For obvious reasons, a national air defence force was in need of such, and in large numbers. As will be laid out below, in the post-war period traditional anti-aircraft artillery initially enjoyed a renaissance of sorts only to be at first supplemented and then completely replaced by guided weapons employing completely new principles.

Post-War Soviet Anti-Aircraft Artillery Development

By the end of the Great Patriotic War, the Soviets were in possession of a large number of anti-aircraft guns, the most numerous of which were 1939-pattern 85mm pieces and 1939-pattern 37mm ones (including derivates thereof). However, it was obvious that these, as well as other types of AA guns in service, were quickly approaching obsolescence.

Post-war challenges necessitated the development of new anti-aircraft guns. In particular, the KS-19 piece of 100mm calibre proved to be a successful design, entering service in large numbers.[1] The gun could engage targets up to an altitude of 15,000 metres and thanks to semi-automation and hydraulic drives (with manual back-ups) a high rate of fire of 14 rounds per minute was attained. Fire control was achieved by means of a SON9 radar (ASCC/NATO-codename 'Fire Can') and PUAZO optical ranged (height-) finder with target data being automatically relayed via cables: up to eight guns could be thus linked forming a battery. Should the need arise, the ability to manually lay the individual guns was maintained. As a side note, the gun could also be used in an anti-tank role as well as a general

A KS-19 100mm anti-aircraft gun in position during an exercise in the 1960s. (Soviet Ministry of Defence)

fire support role and is in fact being utilised for the latter purpose in a number of conflicts up to the present day. Moreover, the piece still remains in limited service in Russia and some other former Soviet republics as an anti-hail gun and to provoke controlled avalanches in mountainous areas.

While the KS-19 gun was a successful design, emerging threats and challenges required a weapon which could reach up to even higher altitudes. This could only be attained by increasing the gun's calibre which resulted in the 130mm KS-30 anti-aircraft gun. Its theoretical engagement altitude was up to 20,600 metres though its effective reach was much less in practice. The gun's design was considerably influenced by captured examples of the German 12.8cm FlaK. While it could be towed, the piece was heavy and required much preparatory work of firing positions. This greatly reduced its mobility making the KS-30 semi-stationary and in fact a large number of these guns were deployed on permanent sites around Moscow as well as other important locations until they were replaced by surface-to-air missiles.

Despite 100mm and 130mm pieces entering service, the need to engage targets at ever higher altitudes was not satisfied. This led

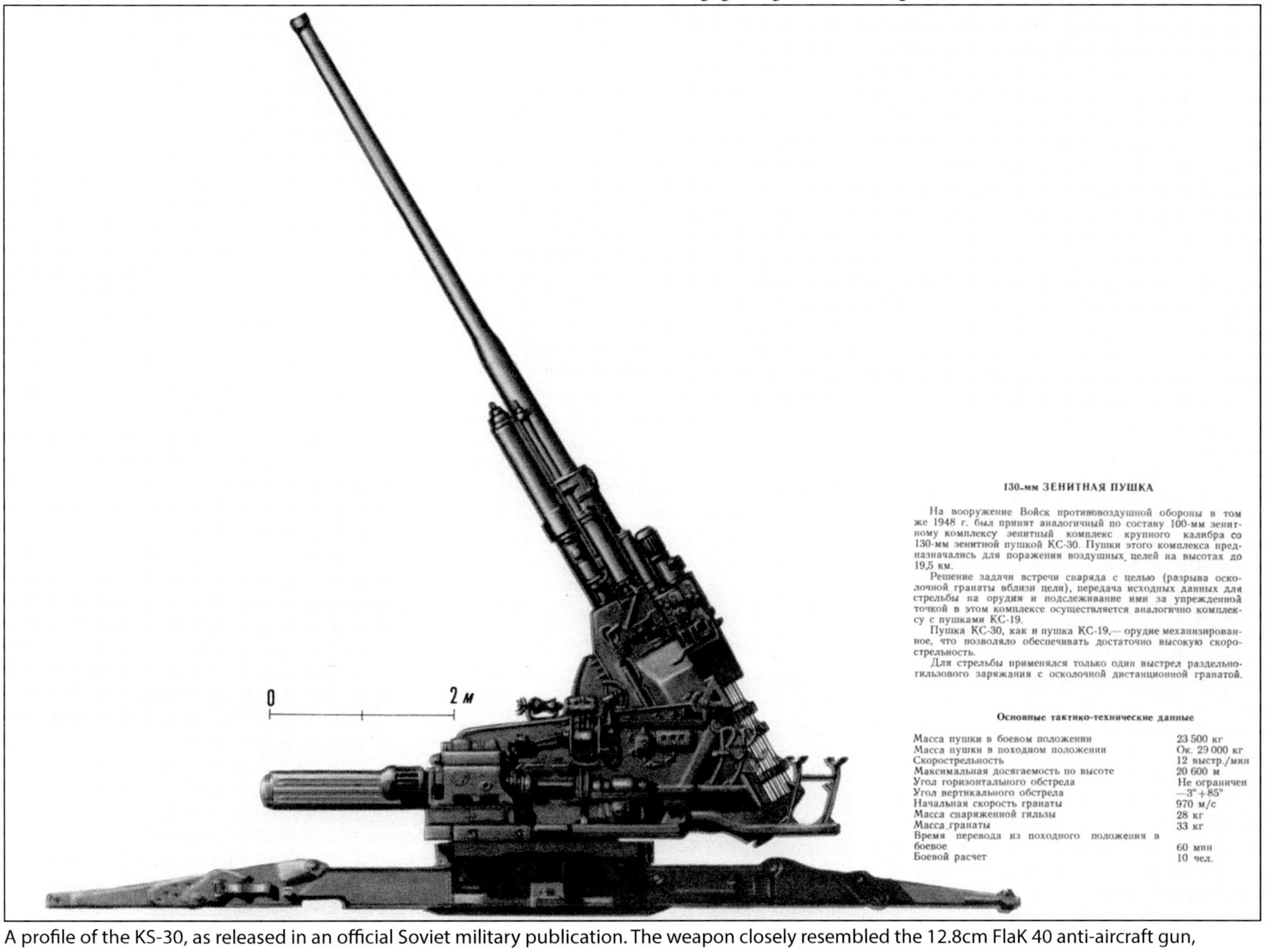

A profile of the KS-30, as released in an official Soviet military publication. The weapon closely resembled the 12.8cm FlaK 40 anti-aircraft gun, developed in Germany during the Second World War. (Soviet Ministry of Defence)

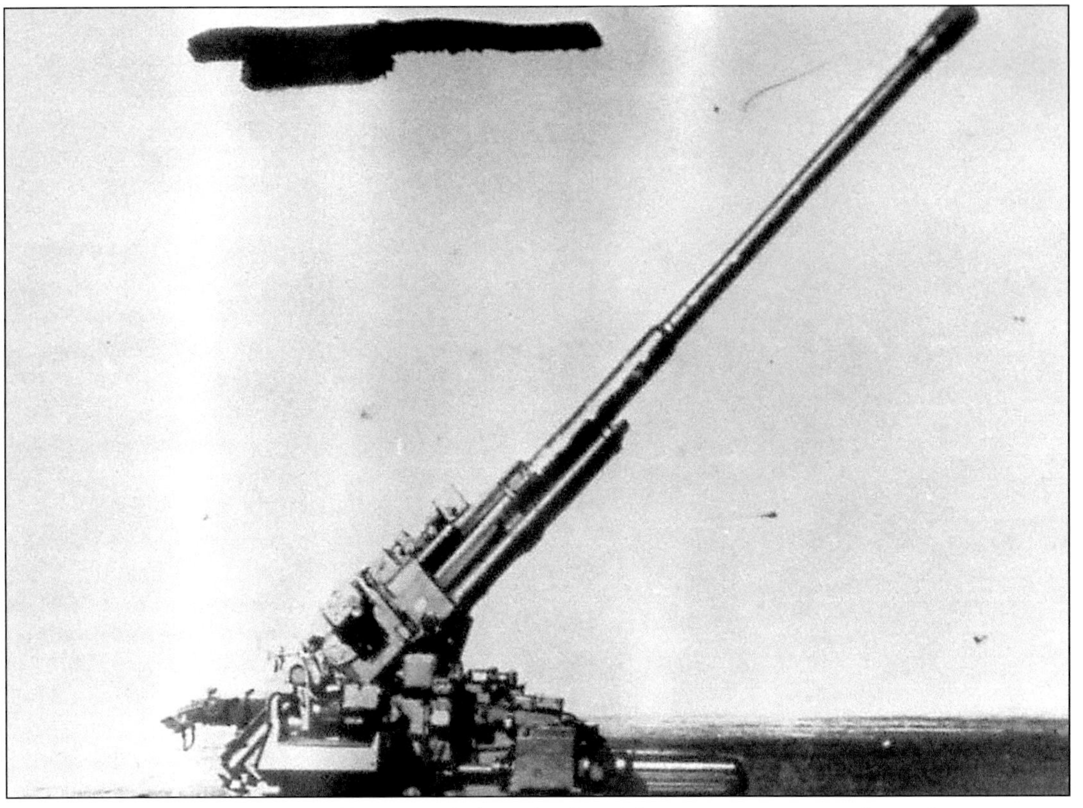

Working from the KS-30, OKB-8 (led by M. Tsyrulnikov), developed the KM-52: an anti-aircraft gun firing projectiles weighing 49kg up to a theoretical altitude of 30,000m. The project was approved and recommended for production in 1955. Only 16 operational pieces (each weighing a staggering 33.5 tons) were delivered by 1967: the weapon was never officially introduced to service because of its inability to reliably target fast moving, jet-propelled aircraft at altitudes of about 10,000 metres. (US DoD)

to the KM-52 anti-aircraft gun of 152mm calibre. Its design drew heavily from that of the KS-30 gun. Theoretically, the KM-52 could fire a shell up to 30,000 metres though its ability to effectively engage targets at high altitudes was limited while it suffered from all the shortcomings which were innate to such a large and heavy piece. As a result, only two batteries of these guns were fielded and set up in defence of Baku. Soon enough, further work on the KM-52 was halted with resources and efforts being concentrated on SAM development instead.

The continuously growing calibre of the weapons described created a gap between medium and heavy AA pieces, and light ones. However, this was soon filled thanks to the introduction of the 57mm S-60 gun. Work on the piece had already started in war time and it was influenced by the captured German 5cm FlaK. When the gun was fielded, it was usually organised in batteries numbering six pieces with fire control being provided by SON (radar) and PUAZO (optical) devices. For its time, the gun was a modern weapon; moreover it was relatively easy to tow, deploy and set up, thus generally earning positive opinions among operators. A twin-barrelled version was used to arm the ZSU-57-2 self-propelled AA gun: the guns were mounted in an open-top turret on a tracked chassis. Both the towed and self-propelled versions of the gun remain in limited service with a number of operators to the present day, though nowadays they are for the most part used as a general fire support weapon.

Last but not least, resulting from the need to replace obsolete Second World War-era small-calibre AA guns, during the time period in question the ZU-23-2 twin 23mm anti-aircraft gun was

The AZP S-60 towed 57mm gun proved effective and highly popular in service. It was manufactured in large numbers and widely exported, and produced under licence in Poland, Hungary, and the People's Republic of China (as the Type 59). (US DoD)

Wasserfall was a simple radio command to line of sight missile, developed in Germany between 1941 and 1944. This photograph shows one during a test launch from the *Prüfstand IX* (Test Site IX) at Peenemünde, in the autumn of 1944. (Bundesarchiv)

being developed, though it entered service only in 1960. Combining good characteristics with ease of operation, it was appreciated by its operators, and still is, for it remains in widespread service in the former Soviet Union as well as throughout the rest of the world.

Even a brief description of Soviet efforts clearly demonstrates that they were striving to develop multiple anti-aircraft gun types of various calibre with an emphasis on medium and heavy examples capable of reaching targets operating at high altitudes. Yet the era of traditional anti-aircraft artillery as the main ground-based air defence weapon was coming to an end. Such could neither offer the reach needed nor ensure a high probability of hitting the target – crucial requirements when combating high-flying reconnaissance aircraft and bombers, especially due to the fact that the latter could carry nuclear bombs. For this, weapon systems of an entirely new kind were needed and were in fact being actively worked on.

Early Soviet Surface-to-Air Missile Development

Since anti-aircraft artillery could not provide the desired level of effectiveness against strategic bombers and other aircraft operating at high altitudes, different means to deal with such threats had to be devised. The latter were already beyond a theoretical stage and slowly morphing into practical solutions. Before moving on, it is first imperative to point out that during the Second World War, the Axis powers were subjected to destructive aerial attacks by Allied heavy bombers. Even though on more than one occasion they managed to inflict heavy losses to the attackers' via conventional air defences, by utilising fighters as well as anti-aircraft artillery, they failed to stop the Anglo-American aerial onslaught. New weapons were clearly needed and such were being worked on by the Germans; to be precise they were developing several models of guided surface-to-air missiles: *Wasserfall, Schmetterling* and *Rheintochter* being the most advanced projects. None of those managed to reach operational status before the war's end; however, considerable work on them had already been performed by that time and when the Soviets overran large parts of Germany, much of it fell into their hands. Initially, the Soviets worked on furthering SAM development on-site in Germany but due to a number of considerations they decided to relocate it to the USSR itself. The move involved not only everything of material value such as missiles and their parts, equipment, machinery and so on, but also the German specialists, who were given 'an offer they could not refuse' and forced to leave for the Soviet Union literally at gun point. Of the three German SAM designs, the *Rheintochter* was abandoned first but work on the *Wasserfall* and *Schmetterling* continued to the point where the missiles were 'cloned' and test fired by the Soviets. In the end, no Soviet versions of any of the German surface-to-air missiles progressed beyond the point of tests and the German specialists were eventually also sent home. But it was not all in vain – on the contrary, in the process the Soviets gained invaluable knowledge which formed a solid base for their own indigenous SAM development.[2]

The need for the aforementioned weapon system gained urgency with the outbreak of the Korean War and it was Stalin's will that it be developed and deployed to defend Moscow as soon as possible.[3] Accordingly, the Soviet Council of Ministers decreed this to be done on 9 August 1950.[4] The task was entrusted to KB-1 (formerly SB-1) headed by Sergo (Sergey) Beria who was the son of Soviet secret police chief Lavrentiy Beria. Not surprisingly, all that was needed for the project's rapid progress was made available without delay. Considerable assistance, particularly with the design of the guidance system, was rendered by German specialists before they were sent home.[5] Having said that, the bulk of the work had to be done by the Soviets themselves and indeed they spared no effort. As a result, tests of the system initially designated *Berkut*, which was subsequently changed to S-25 (the name *Sosna* was also used), commenced on 2 November 1952.[6] Its workability was proven when on 26 April 1953 (the date 25 May also being given),[7] a Tu-4 (a Soviet 'clone' of the American B-29; ASCC/NATO-codename 'Bull') remotely controlled target aircraft was shot down over the Kapustin Yar missile test range. The initial series of tests was concluded on 18 May 1953, by which time a total of 81 test-firings had been undertaken. Additional tests were conducted in September and October 1953, and the first complete S-25 system in an operational configuration was built at Kapustin Yar in January 1954: by 1 April 1955, another series of tests numbering 69 launches at Ilyushin Il-28 and Tu-4 unmanned aerial targets, including a simultaneous launch of 20 missiles against 20 targets, was conducted.[8]

V-300 missiles of the S-25 Berkut SAM system seen during one of the May Day parades in Red Square in Moscow. (Albert Grandolini Collection)

After Stalin's passing in 1953, Beria (the senior one) was executed and while his son was spared such a drastic fate he lost his position, being replaced by Aleksandr Raspletin. Meanwhile S-25 testing was already in full swing and its deployment around Moscow was prepared. The latter was a massive undertaking: the missiles were to have numerous permanent sites with launchpads, bunkers for guidance radars, technical support facilities, barracks for troops, housing for officers and last but not least, roads linking those facilities into one system.[9] In order to command and administrate all of this, a separate air defence army was created, which was operationally divided into four air defence corps which in turn were composed of a number of missile regiments. The combat core of a missile regiment was its missile battalion (*division* in Soviet nomenclature) which operated the actual surface-to-air missile launch site. All missile sites had the same basic configuration with 60 fixed launch pads: three at each of the 20 sideroads which branched off, 10 to each side of the main road running through the centre of the site, with a perimeter road around it. Missiles, which were of a single-stage design powered by a liquid-fuel rocket motor, were towed on semitrailers to the launch pads and once there were raised vertically into the firing position. At a distance from each

A V-300 missile raised on its semi-trailer into the firing position. (Soviet Ministry of Defence)

A test launch of two V-300s from Kapustin Yar, in early 1954. (Albert Grandolini Collection)

launch site, a bunker was constructed housing fire control and guidance electronics with the B-200 radar's characteristic triangular antenna placed on the outside. When identified by the West, what the ASCC/NATO codenamed the 'SA-1 Guild' was assigned to the surface-to-air missile system as a whole and Yo-Yo specifically for its guidance radar.

In all, 56 SAM sites of the type described were built, forming two rings around Moscow: 22 sites constituted the inner ring and the remaining 34 the outer one. The former had a radius of around 50 kilometres from Moscow's city centre while the latter was around 90 kilometres, though the actual distance varied somewhat for each of the sites. Operationally, the sites (and the regiments operating them) from both rings were subordinate to four AD corps, each covering one direction of approach (counter-clockwise north, west, south and east) to the Soviet capital. Early warning was provided by 10 A-100D Kama radar sites, more or less evenly placed around Moscow in a radius of around 300 kilometres from the outer SAM ring. In addition, there was an inner ring of radar sites constituting four A-100B Kama radars at about 25 to 30 kilometres from the city centre (the Kama radars were given ASCC/NATO-codename 'Gage'). The missiles themselves were serviced and stored at large technical support facilities with seven such being built. In order to link all of this, particularly for the purpose of rapidly moving the missiles to the launch sites, two ring-roads were constructed around Moscow with sideroads branching off to the individual sites, facilities and so on. Finally, an airborne component of the system was also worked on as separately described in the sub-chapter dealing with early Soviet air-to-air missile development, but in the end, it failed to enter service.

All the SAM sites were commissioned by the first half of 1955, with the system officially entering service with the Soviet armed forces on 7 May 1955.[10] However, the deployment of actual missiles proceeded at a slow pace and when they were brought to the SAM sites they were not ready for immediate launch. Likewise, the personnel operating the system performed their duties in the manner of a leisurely peacetime routine. All this changed after Moscow was overflown by an American U-2 reconnaissance aircraft on 5 July 1956 (more on this below). Not long after that, the system was brought to actual full combat readiness with 'live' missiles, ready to be fired at a moment's notice, standing on the launchpads. However, the S-25 had missed its chance to prove itself and as far as it is known, the system never again had the opportunity to be used in actual combat despite a long service life. Indeed, the S-25 underwent a number of upgrades and soldiered on into the 1980s, with the last elements of the system being dismantled in the 1990s after the USSR's dissolution. The SAMs themselves were for the first time publicly demonstrated during the 7 November 1960 celebrations of the October Revolution (Bolshevik coup) and would, over the next two decades, take part in numerous military parades.

Fielding the S-25 was a major achievement, but also a cyclopean effort that resulted in an immense drain of resources that could not be repeated anywhere else. This was obvious even before work on the S-25 was completed. For this reason, it became imperative to develop another weapon system of this kind, but one that would be both more economic to manufacture and more flexible to deploy. The Soviet Council of Ministers decreed this to be done on 20 November 1953.[11] Work on the new SAM system was undertaken by a team under Boris Bunkin at the KB-1 bureau and by 1954 its basic design was ready.[12] Development progressed rapidly with the

The result of a successful V-300/S-25 test: the smouldering wreckage of a downed Tu-4 target drone. (Soviet Ministry of Defence)

system's prototype taking shape the next year, followed by initial testing commencing in 1956. The new SAM showed itself to be highly promising with modifications and improvements incorporated into its design when experience gained during tests revealed such to be necessary. Without indulging in a lengthy description of how the development process evolved, it is sufficient to say that it was brought to a successful conclusion with the new SAM system designated S-75 officially entering service on 12 December 1957.[13]

The S-75 was a major improvement over the S-25 in virtually every respect. Its principal components were the V-75 two-staged surface-to-air missile which was fired from a SM-63 single launcher and cued onto the target by a SNR-75 fire control, tracking and guidance unit. Utilising a two-stage missile considerably improved the system's performance vis-à-vis its predecessor; moreover all its components were transportable: the fire control unit was a trailer, the launchers could be fitted with two-wheeled axles and the missiles were placed on semitrailers. Additional radars, cabins for operators, various auxiliary technical equipment and so on were necessary for the system to properly function but all those were also mounted on trucks, trailers or semitrailers. This did not make the system truly mobile, for in order to operate it had to be set up while stationary with both the set-up as well as wind-down being lengthy and laborious. Yet since all its main and auxiliary components were transportable, even if forming a long, heavy and slow train, it made the system re-deployable which was clearly of great advantage. The system's designation was S-75 *Dvina* with subsequent modified variants named S/SA-75 *Desna*, *Volkhov* and *Volga,* named after Russian rivers which became common, though not universal, for Soviet SAMs. When identified by the West, it received the ASCC/NATO-codename 'SA-2 Guideline', while its radar-equipped guidance unit being referred to as 'Fan Song'.

Once accepted into service, large-scale production and deployment of the S-75 began. It was not without problems, resulting in the initial production considerably falling behind the plan: the Soviets intended to manufacture a total of 40 S-75 sites, and 1,200 missiles in 1957, but managed only 30 and 621 respectively.[14] Yet all the

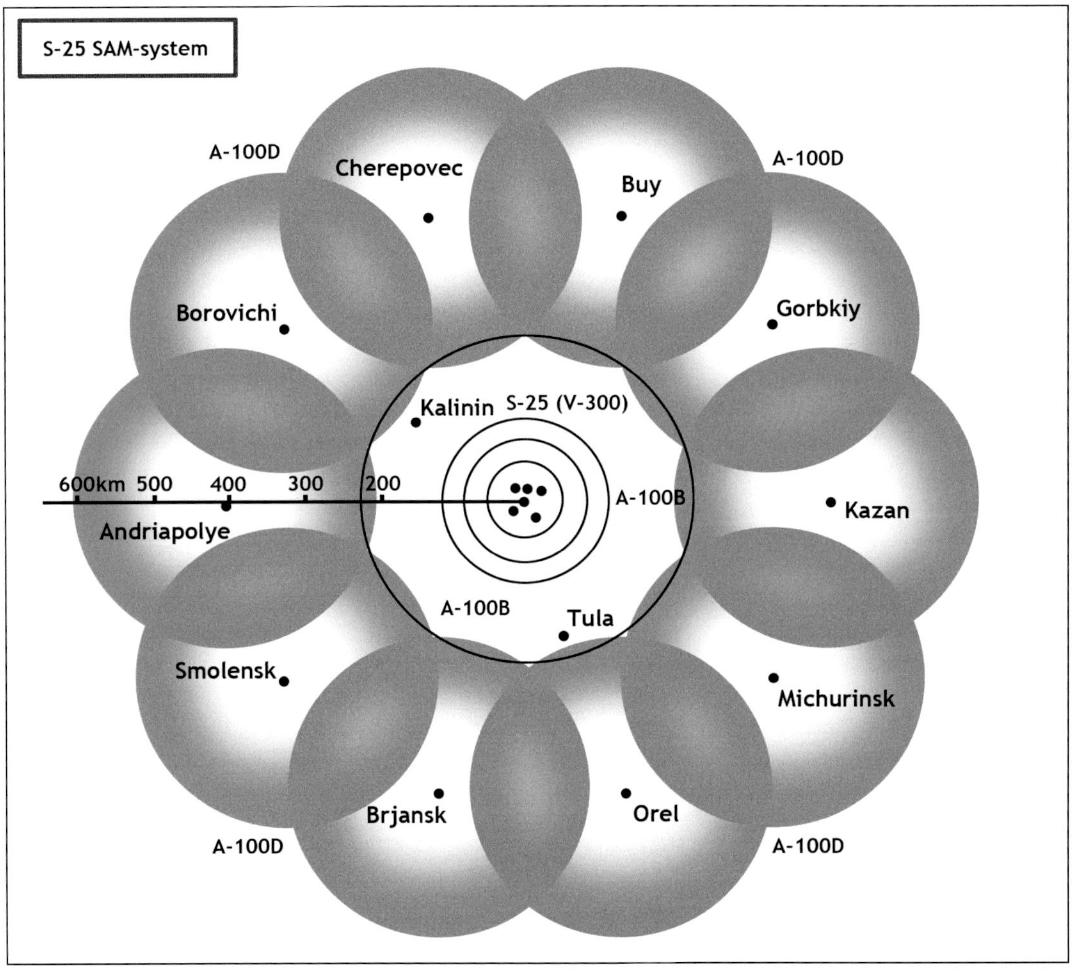

This diagram explains the organisation and composition of the S-25 SAM system, developed and deployed with the sole purpose of protecting Moscow from attacks by strategic bombers. Operated by the 1st Special Purpose Air Defence Army, PVO, this consisted of two 'rings' of S-25/SA-1 SAM sites, A-100B Kama radars, the army headquarters, and headquarters of four subordinated air defence corps (or 'sectors'), distributed in two rings around Moscow. Further outside, 400km away from Moscow was another ring, consisting of A-100D radar sites, each of which had a nominal range of 400km. (Diagram by Tom Cooper)

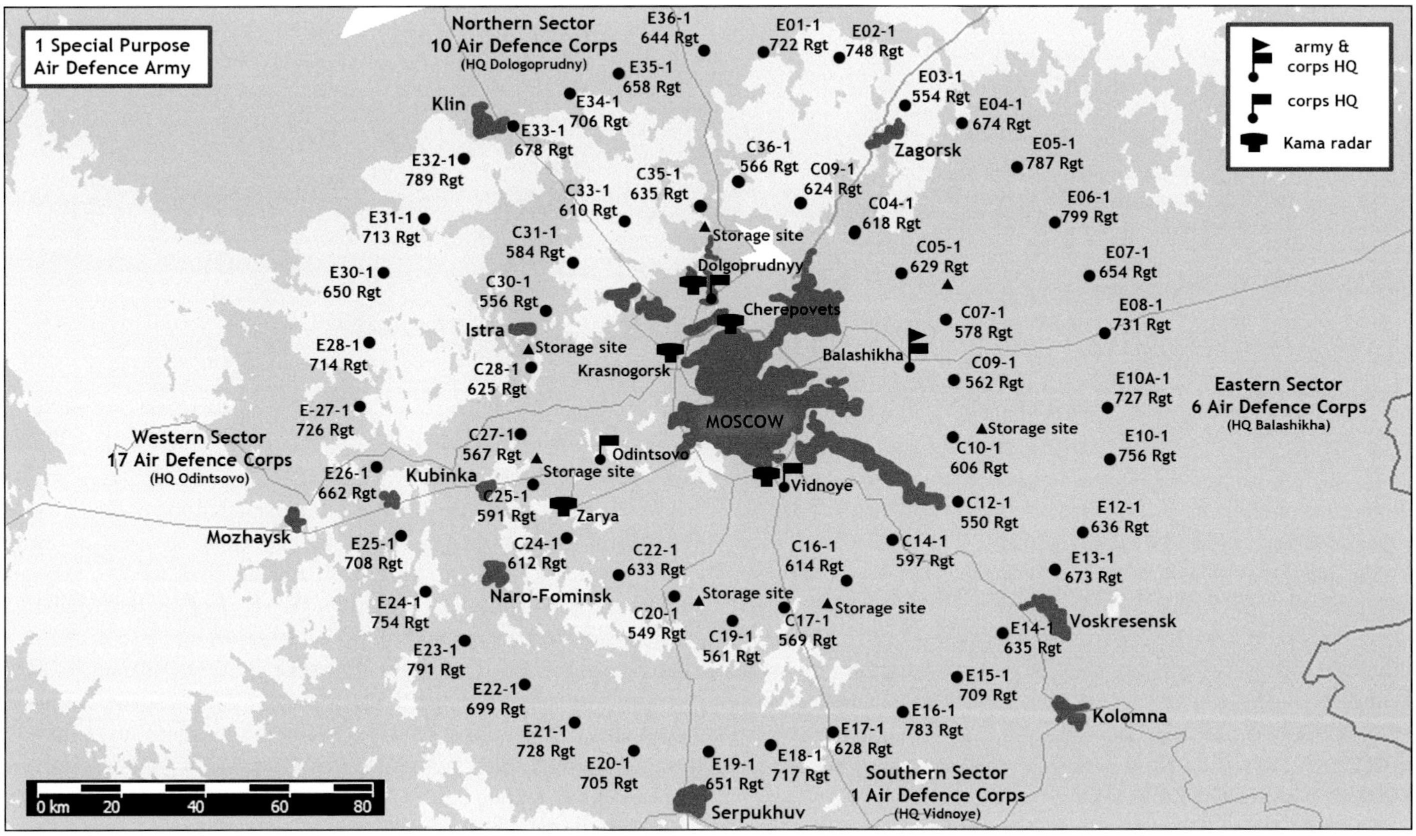

A detailed map of the 'inner rings' of the 1st Special Purpose Air Defence Army, including its army- and corps headquarters, A-100 Kama radar stations in the vicinity of Moscow, its primary units (10th Air Defence Corps, in the north; 6th Air Defence Corps, in the east; 1st Air Defence Corps, in the south; and 17th Air Defence Corps, in the west), and all the known operational SAM sites and regiments as of 1960. (Map by Tom Cooper)

difficulties notwithstanding, more and more population centres, manufacturing facilities, military sites and so on in the Soviet Union were gaining SAM protection. However, it was not only the USSR which needed such defences. Namely, the People's Republic of China, which at that time still enjoyed good relations with the Soviet Union, was experiencing significant problems caused by high-flying reconnaissance aircraft violating its airspace. To deal with it, Beijing requested assistance from Moscow and the Soviets responded swiftly: in late 1958 and early 1959 they delivered five S-75 Dvina SAM systems, one training set, 62 missiles with all the necessary support equipment and sent instructors to train the Chinese in utilising this newly acquired weapons system.[15] Considering that the Soviets were behind schedule in manufacturing SAMs for their own defence and were themselves having a problem with Western high-altitude reconnaissance aircraft penetrating their airspace, the very fact that so much was supplied to the PRC clearly shows the importance they attached to their Asian ally. Soon enough the S-75 proved its worth in 'red' Chinese service, shooting down a ROCAF RB-57D reconnaissance aircraft on 7 October 1959, this being the first ever shootdown of an aircraft by a guided surface-to-air missile

A V-75 missile of the S-75 SAM system, seen on its transporter/reloader, prior to deployment on the launcher. (Albert Grandolini Collection)

A V-75 missile in the process of being loaded onto the launcher. Visible to the left in the rear is a S-75 fire control radar, designated 'Fan Song' in the West. (Albert Grandolini Collection)

under actual combat conditions.[16] It was not long before the Soviets themselves also managed to score SAM kills, as will be related in the pages to follow.

Moving forward to the present day, the S-25 was withdrawn decades ago. Meanwhile, the S-75 still soldiers on with a few operators, being also employed as a surface-to-surface weapon (notably during the ongoing war in Yemen). Interestingly, while neither the S-25 nor the S-75 are in service with Russian air defences in their original role, large numbers of missiles manufactured and stocked for both systems are utilised by the Russians as high-speed aerial targets during air defence live-fire exercises.

Moving back to the 1950s, it should not be forgotten that other projects were also in the works during the time period in question. Among them was *Voron*, a system employing radar for aiming but which fired salvos of unguided rockets, and a rail-mobile SAM system, designated S-50, which would have incorporated many components of the S-25. The latter was intended for the defence of Leningrad (St. Petersburg) as was the *Dal* (400) long-range heavy SAM. None of the systems mentioned entered service, though before being cancelled in 1962 the *Dal* was actually test fired and the construction of its permanent launch sites was also underway (for those reasons it received the ASCC/NATO-codename 'SA-5 Griffon'). In contrast, the S-125 (ASCC/NATO-codename 'SA-3 Goa') which was developed with the intent to engage targets at low and medium altitudes not only entered service in 1961 but proved to have both a long and relatively successful service life which continues to this very day with a number of operators. Apart from surface-to-air missiles, the Soviets also worked on anti-ballistic missile defences and had achieved tangible results already by 1961 which deserves to be related in more detail on a different occasion.

3
EARLY COLD WAR SOVIET MANNED INTERCEPTOR AND AIR-TO-AIR WEAPONS DEVELOPMENT

As much as the initial build-up of traditional anti-aircraft artillery followed by the development and fielding of guided surface-to-air missiles were a vital part of the Soviet air defence effort, it was also obvious that an airborne component of the PVO was indispensable. Accordingly, the Soviets designed and built numerous types of fighter aircraft transitioning from piston-engine propeller-driven ones to jet-powered aircraft able to reach ever higher altitudes and speed. Similarly, their weapons as well as equipment fit underwent a parallel evolution with the introduction of guided air-to-air missiles, on-board radars as well as other electronics which were modern for the time.

Manned Fighter Evolution

Soviet air defence fighter aviation was equipped with various types of aircraft. Of early post-war models the La-11 (ASCC/NATO-codename 'Fang'), which was the last Soviet piston-engine fighter to be fielded in numbers, is particularly noteworthy. Crowning a long line of Lavochkin propeller-driven fighters, it was overall a good design and proved itself in service.[1] Nevertheless, because of the rapid progress of jet-powered flight, it was a mere epigon of a bygone era. Jets were the new focus and here too the Soviets came up with a host of fighter types. Through the late 1940s and 50s the MiG design bureau would introduce ever-improved models at semi-regular intervals. Early ones aside, the MiG-15 (ASCC/NATO-codename 'Fagot'), due to its general performance, manoeuvrability and firepower, was highly rated for its time, being among other things employed in the air defence role – as were the MiG-17 (ASCC/NATO-codename 'Fresco') and the MiG-19 (ASCC/NATO-codename 'Farmer'), the latter becoming the first Soviet supersonic fighter to reach operational status.[2] Initially, the aircraft serving with air defence units differed little from fighters assigned to Frontal Aviation, that is, tactical ones. However, soon it became apparent that to successfully fulfil an air defence role, fighters needed specialised equipment allowing them, for example, to operate at night or in adverse weather conditions. In particular, to make out targets in low visibility, whether that was caused by the onset of darkness or meteorological conditions, MiGs were fitted with radars. Despite the fact that early radar models such as the *Izumrud* (ASCC/NATO-codename 'Scan Odd') had a short detection range and other limitations, they nevertheless equipped appropriately modified versions of the MiG-17 and MiG-19 fighters thus 'branching them off' from the main development line into separate 'families' of air defence fighters. With the fielding of guided air-to-air missiles (see below) MiGs armed with these became dedicated

Crowning the long line of Lavochkin-designed piston-powered fighters, the La-11 was an excellent design that proved itself in service. However, it was an epigon of an era gone by, and the future belonged to jet-powered fighters. (Soviet Ministry of Defence)

fighter-interceptors; however, in the process, they not only lost the capability to be used for any other task but were even limited in their primary role since their gun armament was dispensed with. Due to the fact that early AAMs suffered from various shortcomings, the ability to use a gun should the need arise was soon sorely missed.

Aside from modifying existing fighter models into dedicated air defence interceptors, other aircraft were from the onset designed with this role in mind. Such was the Yak-25 (ASCC/NATO-codename 'Flashlight') which was meant to fill a requirement for a long-range and long endurance interceptor. The aircraft combined several interesting features.[3] Its engines were placed in underwing nacelles which greatly simplified the fuselage structure and did away with the need for an air intake in the nose, thus facilitating the fitting of a radar there. This radar was a *Sokol* (ASCC/NATO-codename 'Scan Three') set which was served by a dedicated radar operator whose station was behind the pilot in a tandem-type two-seat cockpit (both crew stations were fitted with controls allowing the radar operator to pilot the aircraft if necessary). Another interesting feature was the bicycle main landing gear with two supporting outriggers under the wingtips. Its principal armament consisted of two 37mm cannons. In addition, a small number of these fighters, designated Yak-25K, were armed with the RS-2U (ASCC/NATO-codename 'AA-1 Alkali') guided air-to-air missile (other AAMs were tested on the type but not operationally carried). While its performance as well as its range turned out to be below expectations, and the low-hanging engines were prone to damage by foreign object ingestion, it nevertheless was appreciated by aircrews since it had good handling characteristics and was thus relatively easy to fly.[4] The main interceptor model had a comparatively short service life: introduced in the 1950s, its retirement and replacement with

The first Soviet jet fighter taken seriously by the West – and for good reason – was the MiG-15. Developed for intercepting bombers at high altitudes, it had high-performance, was manoeuvrable and unusually heavily armed. (Soviet Ministry of Defence)

A trio of Sukhoi Su-9s overflying Moscow during a parade in the mid-1960s. The type was the first supersonic interceptor in Soviet service capable of not only climbing to altitudes of 20,000m, but effectively operating at those altitudes, and one of the first equipped with RS-2US air-to-air missiles. (Albert Grandolini Collection)

other types had started already in the first half of the next decade. However, the Yak-25's significance lay in that the aircraft with its equipment fit and crew composition was, from the start, designed to fulfil a dedicated air defence interceptor role.

The next logical step in fighter-interceptor development was to design and build not just an aircraft which was more or less suited for the task but a *kompleks* (complex), that is, a weapon system combining a high-performance fighter aircraft with a guided air-to-air missile and onboard radar optimised for that role. Work on this ambitious project codenamed *Anakonda* (anaconda) started in the autumn of 1952: a new, high-performance La-250 supersonic fighter was to be 'mated' with the K-15 weapon system (see below) and everything else necessary for the *kompleks* to come into being.[5] Unfortunately, problems with engine development as well as delays with various other systems forced a major redesign with the La-250 morphing into the La-250A. The latter was only marginally more successful than its predecessor for at least it took off from the ground – in fact several prototypes were build and test flown – but crashes and other accidents as well as further delays finally led to its cancellation in 1959.

One project's failure did not long delay the Soviet efforts to build ever more capable interceptors, especially given that by the mid-1950s both MiG and Sukhoi were working on new swept and delta-winged designs. The former's efforts resulted in the MiG-21 delta fighter (ASCC/NATO-codename 'Fishbed' – work on its swept-wing counterpart was discontinued) while Sukhoi's swept-wing prototype would lead to the Su-7 fighter-bomber (ASCC/NATO-codename 'Fitter') and the delta-winged one to the Su-9 (ASCC/NATO-codename 'Fishpot')[6] fighter-interceptor. The Su-9 proved to be able to actually reach an altitude of 20,000 metres and even higher, as well as a speed of Mach 2, though only for a rather short time on afterburner. It was decided to arm the new interceptor with the RS-2US air-to-air missile, which was a modification of the RS-2U AAM (both received the ASCC/NATO-codename 'AA-1 Alkali'), the primary reason for this being that the weapon was already in service and thus available even though by late 1950s it was becoming obsolete. Unfortunately, the aircraft was not provided with a gun, which considering its missile armament's shortcomings proved to be a poor decision. Still, the Su-9 greatly boosted Soviet air defences capability-wise, not only thanks to its high performance but also due to the fact that as already described it was equipped to work with the ground-based *Vozdukh* target designation and guidance (control) system via the *Lazur* radio command link for automated guidance. Thus, with the Su-9 for the first time a *kompleks perekhvata* (an interception complex or system) was fielded. This integrated a fighter-interceptor and its missile armament with ground-based radar detection, control and guidance into one functional entity capable of intercepting and engaging aerial targets (see above).

The Weapons Fit: Guns and Rockets

Having described early Soviet fighter-interceptor types, it is warranted to devote a few words to their weapons fit. Namely, until air-to-air missiles became the main, or in many cases even the sole, armament of such aircraft, the primary means of engaging the enemy in aerial combat were guns. The Soviet experience from the Second World War was that their fighters were generally lacking firepower, especially when dealing with bombers, which was also matched by what Axis fighter pilots found out: that is, Allied heavy bombers, while not indestructible, proved to be able to absorb considerable punishment. For those reasons, the Soviets preferred cannons of relatively large calibre firing explosive shells with each one of them producing a hefty destructive effect. Accordingly, the last 'red' piston-engine fighter, the La-11, was armed with three NS-23 guns of 23mm calibre while the MiG-15 and MiG-17 received a combined armament of two 23mm NR-23 cannons as well as a single 37mm N-37 piece; the Yak-25 interceptor had two 37mm N-37L cannons and the supersonic MiG-19 three 30mm NR-30 guns.[7] Thus, Soviet fighters packed considerable punch, yet every choice

A trio of Yak-25 interceptors of the PVO overflying Moscow. As well as their large, bulged noses, covering an intercept radar, their heavy armament, consisting of N-37L cannons, visible as thin light strakes low on the fuselage below the cockpit, is visible. While having a very slow rate of fire, these were necessary to cause sufficient damage to down the large US-made bombers. Installed low under the wing, engines were prone to foreign object damage on the ground. Nevertheless, the type was appreciated by its crews because it had good handling characteristics and was relatively easy to fly. (Albert Grandolini Collection)

involved costs of some sort or another, which in the case of such armament selection meant a lower rate of fire. Let it be noted that in contrast, the Americans and other Western designers generally preferred weapons of a lesser calibre which would fire projectiles of correspondingly smaller destructive power when taken singularly, but ones which could be discharged at a higher rate.

Even having a strong gun armament sometimes would not suffice to bring down a strategic bomber, while such a target, especially if it could carry nuclear weapons, had to be destroyed. For this reason, it was decided to boost the firepower of fighters with unguided rockets. Obviously, it would be very difficult to hit a small and manoeuvring aircraft like a tactical fighter with such rockets; however, a large bomber offered a much better target for a salvo of those projectiles. Correspondingly, the Soviets fielded ARS-57 (subsequently redesignated S-5) rockets of 57mm calibre which could be fired from multi-tube rocket pods carried beneath underwing pylons.[8] Several such pods were developed, with the eight-shot RO-57-8 (ORO-57K) and its derivatives becoming the most commonly used ones. Due to the development of AAMs, the weapon soon lost its importance in the air-to-air role but was repurposed to be utilised against ground targets, launched from UB-16 and UB-32 pods, respectively holding 16 and 32 rockets each.

Development of Early Soviet Air-to-Air Missiles

As much as the two S-25 Berkut SAM rings which were to be set up around Moscow projected an image of impregnability, even before their completion certain shortcomings were obvious. For one thing the system, including its radars, was stationary, meaning that something as simple as a relatively minor technical failure at a critical point in time could result in a gap in its coverage. In addition, should a massed and determined air raid take place, some attackers might be able to penetrate it. The first issue called for a mobile radar platform which could be swiftly deployed to any location if additional radar coverage was required. Because of the second consideration, this platform might as well be armed so as to be able not only to detect but also to engage hostile aircraft should the need arise. Since the whole apparatus had to be deployable at any point in the 'SAM rings', and very quickly too, it became obvious that an appropriately modified aircraft would fit the role best. With those factors in mind, a Tu-4 (B-29 clone ASCC/NATO-codename 'Bull') was chosen for the role.[9] Radar and electronic equipment in those times was large and bulky but this was not a problem since the aircraft selected was itself big and could take a heavy payload. Initially, it was envisioned that the aircraft would have four radomes; with forward and rearward facing antennas as well as up and down looking ones in effect giving it an all-around coverage.

The official blessing for the project was given in 1950 and practical work started the next year. Accordingly, a Tu-4, number 226404, was taken to be appropriately modified. It received three bulbous radar radomes: one in the nose (chin position), one dorsal behind the cockpit and finally a ventral one in place of the bomb bay. An additional antenna protruded to the front above the cockpit,

Still from a documentary showing a test-firing of a G-301 air-to-air missile from a heavily modified Tu-4. For details of the latter, see the colour section. (Soviet Ministry of Defence)

however, a rearward facing radar was not installed. The armament could be carried externally on four sets of attachment struts, two under each wing. The weapon option selected was an air-to-air missile based on the S-25 SAM, which considerably shortened development time. The initial AAM design was designated G-300, which was in essence a scaled down version of the S-25 SAM: the air-launched variant was 0.12 metres smaller in diameter as well as 3 metres shorter. In addition, unlike its ground-launched counterpart, the AAM was to have two side-mounted boosters. The guidance method envisioned for the weapon was radar beam-riding. Soon enough, an improved version designated G-301 was developed which did away with the boosters and instead of beam-riding would have had semi-active radar homing guidance. The whole system's detection range was around 35 kilometres while a missile could be guided up to about 20 kilometres. Considering today's standards this is hardly an impressive engagement envelope but for those times such performance was worthwhile.

By 1952 the modified Tu-4 was ready and it conducted a number of test flights carrying AAM mock-ups. In addition, several Tu-2 (ASCC/NATO-codename 'Bat') were also modified to serve as 'flying laboratories' to test some of the electronic equipment as well as in the role of chase aircraft which were fitted with cameras to record missile launches. The first series of 10 AAM test-firings from the Tu-4 took place in autumn 1952, all of which were ballistic launches, that is, without guidance. A second series of trials took place in summer 1953 and the missiles were fired without guidance too; the purpose of this was to test the workability of the launching system, separation from the launch platform, the flight characteristics of the missile, and so on. Despite promising test results, the project was officially terminated in 1954. It was concluded that the whole idea, even if it apparently could be made workable, was impractical. What was really needed were AAMs light and compact enough to be carried by high-performance jet-powered fighter aircraft and work on such was already in progress.

A small guided air-to-air missile had been under development since 1951, originally envisioned as armament for the MiG-15 fighter.[10] The weapon which was designated K-5 (RS-1U) was to have a radar beam-riding guidance system. By autumn 1953, work advanced enough to begin trials with the first test launch from a MiG-17 fighter being performed on 8 October that year. It still took considerable time before the missile became a workable weapon system but on 8 March 1955 a live example was successfully tested against an aerial target. Despite known shortcomings, the military insisted on introducing the weapon into service – and got its wish fulfilled – reasoning that a guided air-to-air missile system

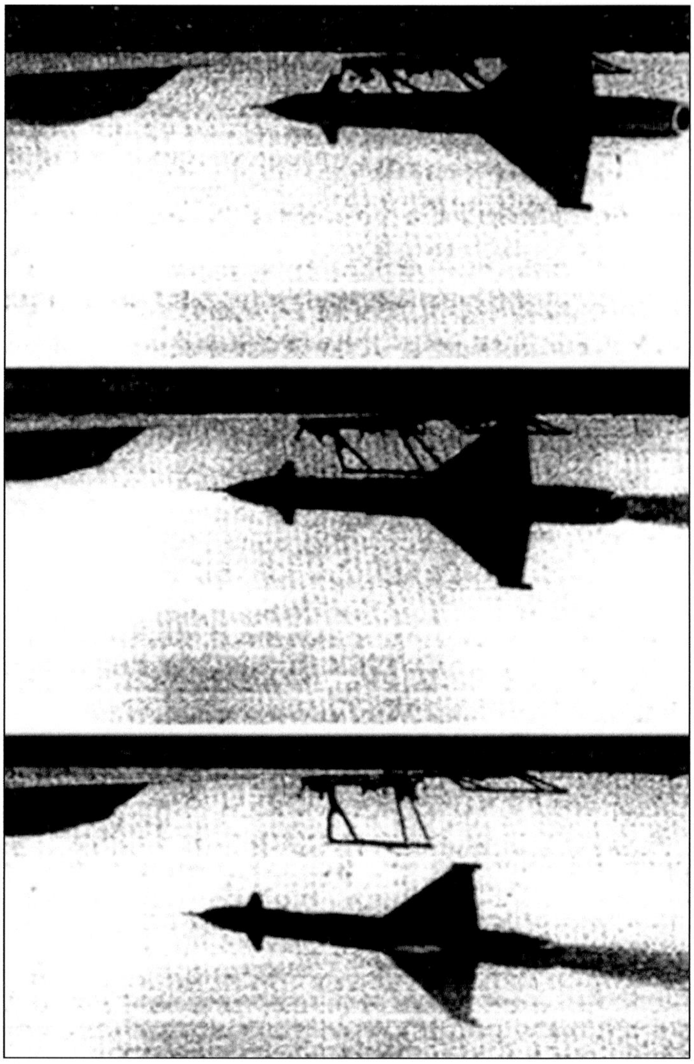

Three frames from a film shown the release of a G-301 from a Tu-4 and its activation. (Soviet Ministry of Defence)

which was far from perfection was better than none at all. Thus, from 1956 onwards, MiG-17 fighters appropriately modified with *Izumrud* radar and four underwing pylons with launch rails were armed with the AAM. While the missile's initial model was still under development, work on a modified version started. Designed specifically as the primary armament for an interceptor variant of the MiG-19 fighter, the weapon designated K-5M (RS-2U) was tested in summer 1957. It had entered service by the autumn of that year, arming the MiG-19PM interceptor as well as a small number of Yak-25Ks. By the late 1950s the AAM in question was technologically obsolete but its availability once more trumped other considerations as it was selected to arm the newest Su-9 interceptor. For this purpose, yet another improved version of the missile designated K-5MS (RS-2US) was fielded. It was visually distinguishable from earlier variants by its larger control surfaces. The missile could also be used by MiG-21 fighters being guided to the target by means of a *Sapphire* (ASCC/NATO-codename 'Spin Scan') radar.

All versions of the missile shared the same basic configuration and radar beam-riding guidance (subsequently an infrared variant was also developed) as well as the same ASCC/NATO-codename 'AA-1 Alkali'. Apart from its short range, the weapon system's primary deficiency was its guidance method, which required the launching aircraft to be almost perfectly aligned to allow the missile to 'ride' the radar beam until it struck the target. This in turn meant that virtually any manoeuvre of the potential victim could break the guidance sequence causing the missile to fly off target. As a side

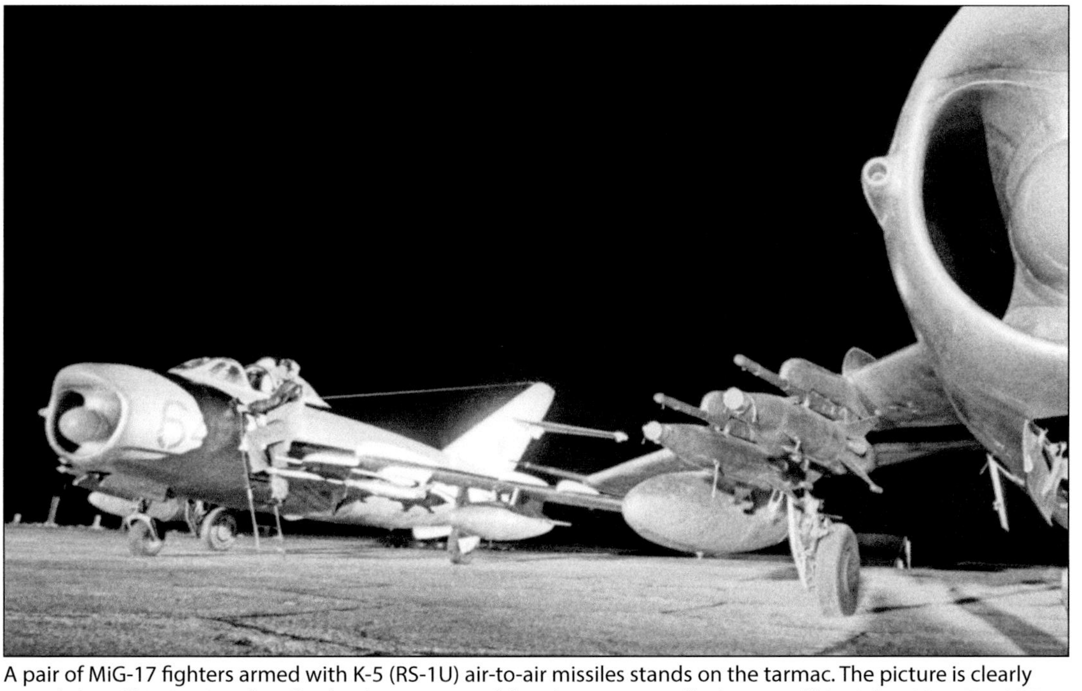

A pair of MiG-17 fighters armed with K-5 (RS-1U) air-to-air missiles stands on the tarmac. The picture is clearly posed since illuminating the pilot for the purpose of the photo temporally destroyed his night vision. The MiG-17PFU was the first Soviet fighter armed with AAMs to enter service in numbers. (Albert Grandolini Collection)

A line-up of MiG-19PM fighters with their primary armament the K-5M (RS-2U) AAMs in the foreground. The type pictured was the first Soviet missile-armed supersonic interceptor. (Albert Grandolini Collection)

note, it may be added that the weapon could also be used in the air-to-surface role but due to its short range and small warhead such a use was deemed impractical.

Soviet efforts to develop AAMs were unexpectedly boosted when American GAR-8 (subsequently redesignated AIM-9B Sidewinder) infrared guided missiles were acquired via the People's Republic of China. The US air-to-air missiles were rushed to the Republic of China (Taiwan) by the Americans in the autumn of 1958 to help the ROCAF fend off numerically superior 'red' Chinese MiGs.[11] In the course of the resulting aerial engagements, a number of GAR-8 missiles were fired, one of which struck a MiG without exploding and was brought back to base. In addition, three more American AAMs (the remains thereof) which failed to hit home were recovered by the People's Liberation Army, which ordered large units of its troops to comb mainland Chinese coastal areas near Taiwan – the 'red' Chinese clearly demonstrated they knew how to effectively utilise their vast manpower![12] Recovered US missile technology was transferred to the Soviet Union where it was carefully studied and copied. The Soviets were surprised by some of the American technical solutions and had to master new technologies in order to 'clone' the US missile. For obvious reasons these efforts received a high priority and by the end of 1959 a Soviet copy of the missile was successfully tested. Early in 1960, the new AAM was put into production under the designation R-3 (K-13) and once identified by the West it received the ASCC/NATO-codename 'AA-2 Atoll'. The missile became the primary air-to-air weapon of the MiG-21 fighter and was subsequently used to arm other types of Soviet fighters and fighter-bombers.

The Soviets were also working on a number of other guided air-to-air missiles which either became operational at a later date or failed to progress beyond the development stage. Those envisioned for the failed La-250 and 250A interceptors deserve a mention. Designated K-15, these AAMs evolved together with the aircraft they were supposed to arm.[13] The first version, with the index 275, was to have a range of around 15 kilometres, radar beam-riding guidance and would be carried semi-recessed under the La-250's fuselage. When the latter morphed into the La-250A, so did the missile, becoming the 275A. Work on the weapon, with meanwhile considerably improved characteristics, progressed to the point that full sized mock-ups were built and carried beneath the wing pylons of La-250A prototypes. In addition, three more variants were in various stages of design: the 277, 279 and 280 missiles, of which the 279 was to have a nuclear warhead. However, when work on the La-250A interceptor was terminated, development of the missiles it was supposed to be armed with was halted as well.

Closing the subject of Soviet post-war and early Cold War air defence development, it is warranted to point out that the efforts undertaken up to that time were not always successful or yielded results that could be deemed satisfactory. Yet with only a number of caveats, it still stands that within just 15 years from the end of

The Su-9 – the crowning achievement of Soviet fighter-interceptor development in the 1950s – was Mach-2 capable and could carry up to four AAMs. Due to the fact that the type was equipped to work with the ground-based *Vozdukh* target designation and guidance (control) system via the *Lazur* radio command link for automated guidance, the first *kompleks perekhvata* (interception complex/system) was fielded. As a side note Soviet jet engines tended to be fuel thirsty while the expanses to be covered were immense and thus external fuel tanks such as those visible installed under the centreline were an almost permanent fixture. (Albert Grandolini Collection)

The first prototype of the ill-fated La-250, armed with a pair of K-15 air-to-air missiles. (Soviet Ministry of Defence)

An R-3S infrared homing, short-range, air-to-air missile (ASCC/NATO-codename 'AA-2 Atoll'). The weapon was a copy of the US-made GAR-8 (later AIM-9B Sidewinder). While enabling a giant leap forward for the Soviet missile manufacturers, and produced in immense numbers, it saw relatively little service with interceptors operated by the PVO. (National Airspace Museum)

the war until 1960, the Soviet air defence fighter fleet went from being equipped with gun-armed, piston-engine propeller-driven aircraft to having ones capable of reaching a speed of Mach 2 and launching AAMs. Similarly, ground-based air defences were steadily moving away from traditional anti-aircraft guns to guided surface-to-air missiles and the radar network was greatly expanded and its integration was also begun. Last but not least, all the above was just the beginning as far as the Soviet development of high-performance interceptors, guided air-to-air missiles, automated control systems, SAMs and so on was concerned.

4
THE GAME IS ON

For reasons already outlined, the onset of the Cold War was also the onset of US aerial reconnaissance of the Soviet Union. As early as 1946 the then-United States Army Air Force (USAAF, reorganised as the US Air Force, USAF, and thus an independent branch of the US armed forces in 1947) started to conduct its Peacetime Airborne Reconnaissance Program (PARPRO), which included operations along the Soviet borders – but not penetrations of Soviet airspace.[1]

Arguably, the first 'real' Cold War reconnaissance missions were those conducted in the course of Operation Nanook. Its aim was, among other things, to gather data for Strategic Air Command (SAC) concerning the shortest route to the Soviet heartland over the North Pole. For that purpose, in June 1946, the 46th Reconnaissance Squadron was established at Ladd Field outside of Fairbanks, Alaska. The squadron's first operational mission was flown on 2 August 1946.[2] Soon enough, more intelligence-gathering operations commenced. Amongst them was Project 20, the purpose of which was the photographing of Soviet naval vessels, aircraft and any 'unusual object or activity'. Furthermore, Project 23 involved two aircraft with one configured for electronic intelligence (ELINT) and the other for imagery intelligence (IMINT), which flew along the Siberian coast. This intelligence-gathering activity did not escape Soviet attention: following a 22 December 1947 Project 23 sortie, the Soviets issued a diplomatic protest alleging that an American aircraft violated Soviet airspace 'for about seven miles along the coast of the Chukotski Peninsula at a distance two miles from the shore.'[3] According to US sources, the first mission involving the intentional penetration of Soviet airspace took place on 5 August 1948.[4] It appears the highest level of authorisation it had was from General Karl Spaatz who, after the creation of the independent Air Force by the National Security Act of 1947, was appointed as the first Chief of Staff USAF in September 1957. Using a stripped-down RB-29 (RF-13A) of the 46th Reconnaissance Squadron, they flew into Siberia at an altitude of 35,000 feet, that is, above 10,000 metres. The mission lasted well over 19 hours and its purpose was to ascertain if the Soviets were concentrating their bombers for a surprise attack against the United States – theoretically they would be capable of reaching the US by performing a one-way only mission but the damage they could inflict was limited to conventional bombardment since the Soviet nuclear bomb was at that time still under development. Fortunately, no preparations for a Soviet attack were made out and the added bonus of the mission was that detailed images of Soviet installations, including radar sites, as well as of littoral areas were obtained.

For the record let it be noted that Russian sources on their part assert that the first American overflight of Soviet territory took place as early as 5 April 1946 when two US aircraft flying from Iran penetrated six kilometres into the USSR's airspace.[5] Obviously, that was not a deep penetration but just a shallow incursion, yet it was an incursion nonetheless. In any case more overflights, collectively known as SENSINT (Sensitive Intelligence), followed, with the first acknowledged one taking place on 10 May 1949, when a RF-80A with 1st Lieutenant Bryce Poe II at the controls flew over Soviet military airfields on the Kurile Islands.[6] Between March and August 1950, RF-80 reconnaissance aircraft based in Japan performed 19 additional SENSINT overflights including missions over Sakhalin Island, the Kurile Islands, as well as the Soviet mainland around Vladivostok. The purpose of all of these missions was to obtain information regarding the strength of the Soviet Air Force in the Far East. Apart from the US Air Force, the US Navy also got into the 'business' of reconnoitring the Soviets from the air but they had a somewhat improvised start.[7] Namely, when it was decided to equip two patrol squadrons to conduct the electronic reconnaissance missions, it transpired that there was insufficient equipment on hand. In order to quickly remedy the situation, two US Navy chief electronic technicians were sent out to locate and buy back equipment which previously had been sold as surplus! In civilian apparel and carrying large quantities of cash, the two chiefs purchased all the intercept receivers, direction finders, pulse analysers and other electronic reconnaissance equipment they could find. This equipment was then installed in PB4Y Privateers and P2V Neptunes for the purpose of electronic reconnaissance missions around the periphery of the communist nations, particularly the Soviet Union.

Apart from those described above, a number of other reconnaissance missions both singular as well as within programs (projects) were also flown. Such missions occasionally resulted in the penetration of the USSR's airspace which were either accidental or – less frequently – deliberate. It should be underscored that in the late 1940s it was a general US policy to avoid the latter. Despite requests for authorisation to not only reconnoitre peripheral areas but to conduct overflights directly of Soviet territory itself, the Joint Chiefs of Staff, after consulting with among others the Secretary of Defence and the Secretary of State, repeatedly denied such overflights.[8] Nevertheless, US aerial reconnaissance activity from time to time resulted in a diplomatic protest from the Soviets while their military response was negligible with few attempts at interception. This is hardly surprising for due to insufficient radar coverage many reconnaissance missions were not detected at all and even if they were, the Soviet fighter force was composed for the most part of obsolete – or close to it – piston-engine types and was limited in its capabilities.

In addition, it deserves to be noted that the Americans were not the only ones to reconnoitre Soviet airspace. Between 1947 and 1950, the Royal Air Force of Great Britain (RAF), and the Norwegian and Swedish air forces made a number of overflights, which were for the most part shallow, over northern Soviet territories and the island of Spitsbergen (which was under partial Soviet control) utilising photoreconnaissance equipment provided by the United States.[9] The photographic intelligence gathered in the course of those missions was shared with the Americans. Moreover, the Swedish air force also performed a number of reconnaissance missions in the Baltic which were prompted by reports of rockets flying through Swedish airspace. Initially, most missions were unsuccessful as Soviet fighters intercepted the Swedish reconnaissance aircraft long before they could reach their objectives, leaving them with no option but to turn back.[10] However, once operations were switched to night time it proved possible to fly reconnaissance sorties along the Soviet Baltic coast, though major cities were avoided.[11]

As far as it is known, the aforementioned overflights did not result in any noteworthy incidents. Elsewhere, a relatively minor incident did possibly happen when an aircraft claiming to be an 'Iranian P-5', supposedly landed on 27 March 1947 about 25 kilometres from Dzhulfa (in those days Sovetskaya Dzhulfa) in Azerbaijan.[12] According to the Soviets, its crew constituted two men who were identified as pilot Lieutenant Sabir Muagasi and observer Junior Lieutenant Safari Husein, who were detained.[13] Reportedly the Iranians claimed to have become disoriented and since no malicious intent could be proven by the Soviets, the aircraft as well as both men were subsequently released to Iran. A few years later, on 3 August 1951, a formation of Turkish aircraft violated Soviet airspace over Armenia, allegedly approaching Leninakan (present day Giumri) before turning back.[14] In this case it appeared to have been a deliberate act; however, apart from spotting the intruders, the Soviets were not able to mount an effective response.

First Blood?

Possibly the first Cold War aerial victory achieved by the Soviets against a foreign aircraft carrying out a purposefully malevolent mission in the USSR's airspace took place in autumn 1949. Reportedly an aircraft identified as a B-25 dropped three parachutists in the vicinity of Kirovograd (present day Kropyvnytskyi in Ukraine) but was intercepted and shot down by Soviet fighter aircraft over the Black Sea not far from Odessa. Surviving crewmembers were rescued from the water and taken into captivity by a Soviet patrol vessel.[15] Unfortunately, available sources are silent on such important details as, for example, the exact date of the incident mentioned. Yet it is not just theoretically possible but very much plausible that this shootdown indeed occurred. The CIA conducted a number of intelligence-gathering operations involving the parachuting of agents into Eastern Bloc countries as well as the Soviet Union itself. It can be ascertained from declassified documents that among these was Operation Aerodynamic which aimed to airdrop infiltrators into Soviet Ukraine.[16] For the purpose of such undertakings aircraft were utilised that were not in the inventory of the United States Air Force, which was easily made possible by the abundance of surplus aircraft of various types after the Second World War ended. The said aircraft were crewed by expatriates, with the agents who were airdropped also being recruited from emigree communities in the United States and elsewhere in the West. It needs to be pointed out that after the war, a large number of people hailing from the Soviet Union, as well as countries which fell under Soviet dominance, found themselves stranded on the 'wrong' side of the Iron Curtain. Many either could not or were unwilling to return to their home countries by normal means and were ready to take considerable personal risk to actively oppose Sovietism and Communism which they – not without reasons – blamed for their woes. Thus, the CIA as well as other Western intelligence agencies had both aircraft and men whom they could use in high risk missions without having to consider the backlash which, as subsequent events proved, was sure to come if Americans and aircraft in the inventory of the US Air

Force, Navy or otherwise officially in the inventory of an American agency were to be lost during a mission in or around Soviet airspace. Bearing that in mind, it is not hard to conclude that while not proven beyond doubt, it is realistically possible for an aircraft with its crew to have fallen prey to Soviet defences in 1949. If so, this loss was written off by the United States without official acknowledgement, since the men and the aircraft could be plausibly considered not to be American and thus were treated as expendable Cold War cannon fodder. The successful paradropping of agents into the USSR clearly demonstrated how inefficient the Soviet defences were; however the missions were still intelligence failures for – as admitted by the CIA itself – the agents were for the most part killed or captured with some of the latter 'turned' to relay back false information.[17]

Turbulent Turtle's Troubles

The 1949 incident – while not beyond the realm of possibilities – remains unconfirmed. Thus, the first undisputed Cold War shootdown of a US – or any Western – aircraft by Soviet fighters in defence of the USSR's airspace took place on 8 April 1950 over the Baltic Sea in the vicinity of Líepaya (present day Liepāja in Latvia). To give some background to the dramatic events which were to unfold, it needs to be pointed out that the Soviets were aware of US aerial reconnaissance activity and as early as 1947 they were protesting alleged airspace violations by US aircraft, while by 1949 American reconnaissance aircraft were already routinely flying in the vicinity of Soviet borders (see above) and, according to the Soviets, were actually intentionally violating their airspace; an accusation which was not entirely baseless. For example, one such violation over Soviet territorial waters reportedly took place on 22 October 1949; an aircraft which was identified by the Soviets as a RB-29 was intercepted by four La-7 fighters which did not attempt to force it to land but instead forced it to fly away, firing warning shots in the process.[18] On that occasion, the situation was resolved with no blood being shed but as subsequent events demonstrated, this would not always be so.

Going back to the events of 8 April 1950; a US aircraft was intercepted by four Soviet La-11 fighters of the 30th GIAP which took to the air from Palanga Air Base (AB) in Lithuania.[19] The Soviet

A La-11 pilot accompanied by the crew chief walks away from his mount after a mission. The scene after Lt. Tezyayev returned to base after shooting down the "Turbulent Turtle" would have not looked much different. (Soviet Ministry of Defence)

A PB4Y-2 Privateer – the same type as 'Turbulent Turtle', shot down on 8 April 1950 – seen underway from Naval Air Station Jacksonville, around the same time. As far as is known, the ill-fated example wore less conspicuous markings, including the tailfin code EB, no service title, no modex number, and had its national marking applied further to the front. The Soviet pilots that intercepted Turbulent Turtle misidentified it as a 'B-29 bomber'. (US DoD)

formation was led by Senior Lieutenant B. Dokin with Lieutenant I. Tezyayev being his wingman, while the remaining two Lavochkin fighters were flown by Senior Lieutenant A. Gerasimov and Lieutenant Ye. Satayev. At 1739 hours Moscow time, an American four-engine aircraft flying at an altitude of 4,000 metres was intercepted some eight kilometres south of Líepaya. The US aircraft, which was misidentified as a B-29, flew a 135° course. Gerasimov and Satayev manoeuvred in front of the American aircraft signalling it to follow them, while Dokin and Tezyayev flew behind it to the right. Instead of following the Soviets, the US aircraft changed its heading to 270˚ setting it on a course towards the open sea. Since the Americans were ignoring Soviet signals and were attempting to fly away instead, Senior Lieutenant Dokin fired warning shots, expending 12 rounds. According to the Soviets, the Americans opened fire on them with their on-board defensive armament, whereupon Lieutenant Tezyayev replied in kind with sustained cannon fire. Having received apparently crippling hits, the obviously stricken US aircraft started to lose altitude, disappearing from view in low-hanging clouds at about 500 metres and it presumably crashed into the sea some five to ten kilometres from the shore. Subsequently the Soviets estimated the position of the crash to be approximately 56°30'0 N, 20°28'0 E.[20] The downing of the US aircraft earned Lieutenant Tezyayev the Order of the Red Star.[21] It is interesting to note that during the Second World War Tezyayev flew US-made P-39 Air Cobra fighters.

So much for the Soviet version of events – perhaps not surprisingly the United States had a slightly different position concerning the matter. At the time of the incident, the Americans maintained that the aircraft, which was unarmed, was conducting a 'training flight' from West Germany to Denmark when it was attacked. A quarter of a century later, in 1975, the Naval Investigative Board report of the incident was declassified and admitted that the aircraft was engaged in a 'special electronic search project mission.'[22] In fact, the lost aircraft was the PB4Y-2 Privateer BuNo 59645, named by its

Ivan Tezyayev in full medal regalia, including the Order of the Red Star he was awarded for shooting down the PB4Y-2 'Turbulent Turtle' on 8 April 1950. All 10 crewmembers of the patrol bomber belonging to VP-26 were presumed killed. (Soviet Ministry of Defence)

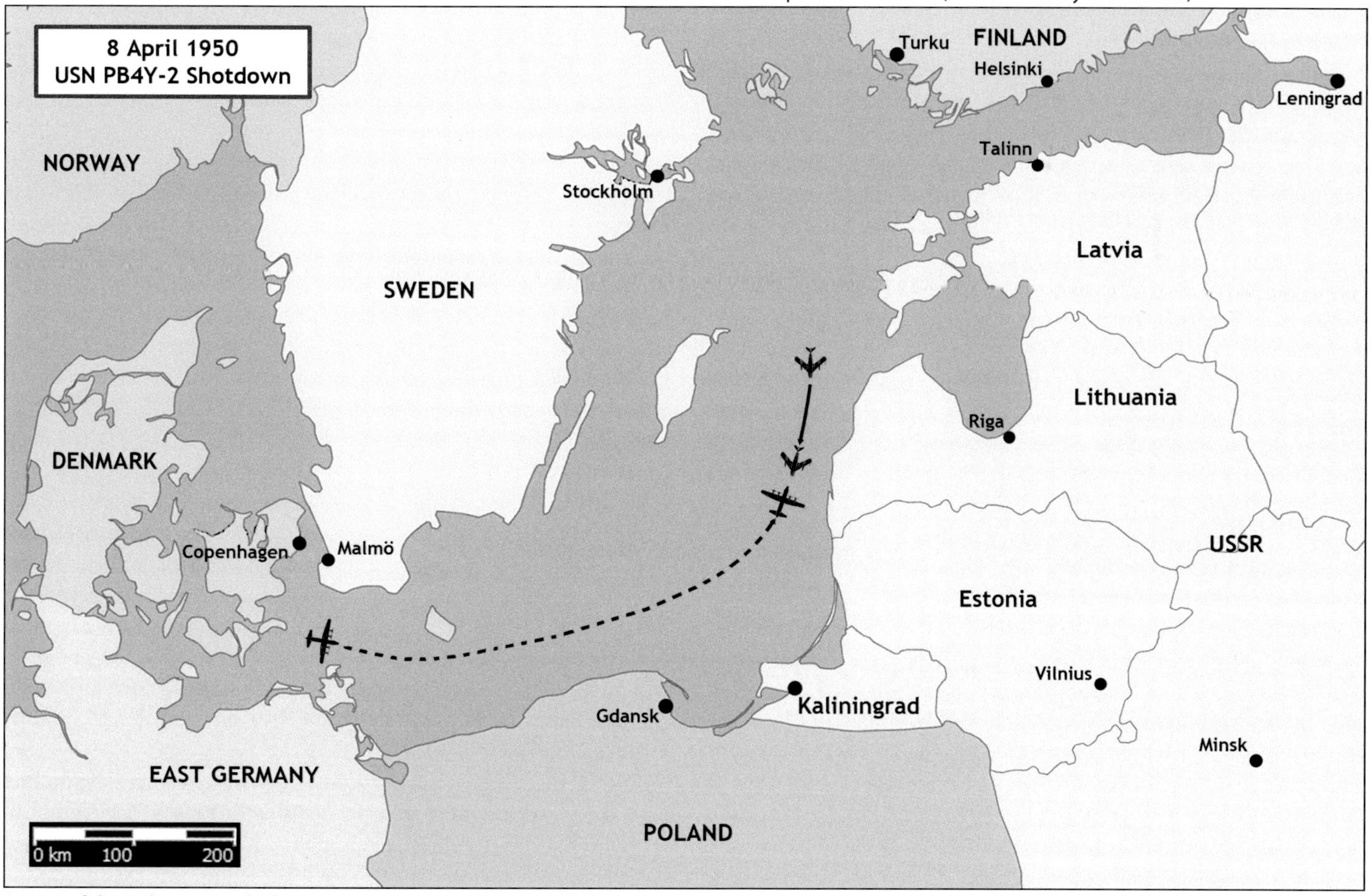

A map of the Baltic Sea with the approximate route flown by the PB4Y-2 Privateer 'Turbulent Turtle' on 8 April 1950. (Map by Tom Cooper)

crew 'Turbulent Turtle', which was part of a secret Special Electronic Search Project detachment assigned to Patrol Squadron 26 (VP-26).[23] It took off from Wiesbaden in West Germany at 1031 hours local time on 8 April 1950. At 1301 hours, BuNo 59645 reported crossing the German coast en route to Copenhagen. This was its last radio transmission. At 2230 hours, the US Air Force Flight Service at Frankfurt, Germany, declared BuNo 59645 overdue.[24] Since the aircraft failed to reach its intended destination, a search and rescue operation was put into motion. While no survivors or bodies were found, some flotsam identified as originating from the aircraft was recovered.[25] Among these items were two life rafts, which combined with subsequent Cold War-era reports and even later post-Soviet sensationalist claims, created the impression that at least some of the Privateer's crewmen might have survived and lived on in Soviet captivity.[26] This appears highly unlikely and the US–Russia Joint Commission on POWs/MIAs (USRJC) which was established in 1992 by the presidents of the United States and the Russian Federation, George H. W. Bush and Boris Yeltsin, failed to confirm claims that the wreckage of the US aircraft was recovered by the Soviets.[27] In any case, the Privateer's entire crew of 10 was listed as deceased. Lest they be forgotten: AT1 Frank L. Beckman, AL3 Joseph J. Bourassa, ENS Tommy L. Burgess, AD 1 Joseph H. Danens, LT John H. Fette, CT3 Edward J. Purcell, LTJG Robert D. Reynolds, AN Joseph N. Rinnier, LT Howard W. Seeschaf, AD 1 Jack W. Thomas. Each of the men was posthumously awarded the Distinguished Flying Cross and in addition a commemorative tablet was put up in Lithuania after it became an independent country. The number of fatalities could have been 11, but one of the crewmen, Technician Stephen J. Zaklan, was left behind at Wiesbaden due to health problems – a lucky man indeed![28]

The demise of the 'Turbulent Turtle' and its crew was the first in a list of different, yet in many ways similar, incidents: a US aircraft would be shot down by Soviet fighters in the vicinity of, or actually inside, Soviet airspace, with the exact circumstances of how such an event came about and the fate of the aircraft's crew being disputed. This would repeat itself throughout the 1950s and less frequently in the following decades until the end of the Cold War.

5
FAR EASTERN FRACAS

In December 1950, US President Harry Truman authorised direct overflights of the Soviet Union.[1] The decision was seen as necessary in view of the outbreak of the Korean War in June that year. Furthermore, the West in general grew increasingly apprehensive concerning the Soviet Union's development of nuclear weapons (the first Soviet atomic bomb was detonated in 1949),[2] strategic bombers, missiles and so on. Thus, American and other Western reconnaissance flights became more intensive and intrusive, which in turn resulted in Soviet aerial defences, fighter pilots in particular, becoming much more assertive. If previously shootdowns or even the firing of warning shots had been singular events, from this point onwards they became more frequent.

Claimed and Confirmed Clashes

An incident resulting from the outbreak of the Korean War occurred soon enough: according to Russian sources a RB-29 was shot down on 26 December 1950 in the vicinity of Cape Seisyur, located at the mouth of the Tumen river (right at the border with North Korea).[3] Supposedly the aircraft fell victim to MiG-15s of the 523rd IAP flown by Captain S. A. Bakhayev and Senior Lieutenant N. Kotov. However, there is no confirmation of a B-29 or RB-29 lost on that date, nor was this incident investigated by the USRJC which would have certainly taken it under its scrutiny if loss of life among US airmen had occurred.[4] The closest that can be taken as quasi-confirmation of something having indeed happened on that date is a laconic mention of a MiG attack against a RB-29 in the history of the Far East Air Forces.[5] The US aircraft involved may have been the RB-29 (44-61855) of the 91st Strategic Reconnaissance Squadron. In addition, according to US sources at an earlier date, 15 July 1950, a USAF B-29 'ferret' was intercepted by Soviet fighters over the Sea of Japan but it escaped unscathed.[6]

Those incidents aside, a confirmed loss of an American reconnaissance aircraft to the Soviets took place on 6 November 1951. That day a P2V Neptune, BuNo 124283 assigned to Patrol Squadron Six (VP-6) stationed at Naval Air Station Atsugi, Japan, took to the air manned by a crew of 10. When four decades later its fate became a subject of USRJC's work, the US side acknowledged that the aircraft had been on an intelligence-gathering mission.[7] This USN aircraft itself did not make any transmissions indicating a Soviet attack, however, American COMINT intercepts showed that the Soviets had shot it down and observed its remains burning on the surface of the sea.[8] That much was soon confirmed by the Soviets themselves who protested the alleged border violation by the US aircraft, further asserting that their fighters had been forced to return fire when the Americans shot at them first. While the notion that a reconnaissance aircraft would provoke such an exchange of fire appears not particularly credible, there seems to be a precedent; sometime between October and December 1950 (the exact date could not be established) a Neptune of VP-6 flew a nocturnal reconnaissance mission coming within about 15 miles of Vladivostok. According to the Americans, four Soviet MiG fighters came up to intercept them, whereupon the Neptune turned back towards its base in Japan. Since the Soviets continued to pursue the USN aircraft, the squadron's commander Arthur F. Farwell, who happened to be aboard the Neptune, first ordered the rear gunner to stand by and then to give a five-second burst right at the Soviet fighters if they came too close. Apparently one of the Soviet pilots did just that and the rear gunner Chief S. L. Whitson fired a burst at him from the Neptune's 20mm tail gun. As a result, the Soviet fighter exploded in mid-air. Not waiting for the remaining trio of MiGs to join the fight, the Neptune entered into a dive and made good its escape at low level.[9]

While the author failed to find a Soviet loss corresponding with the above claim, it nevertheless demonstrates that American reconnaissance aircraft were not always passive when intercepted. Reverting to the events of 6 November 1951, the USN Neptune BuNo 124283 was shot down by Senior Lieutenants I. Ya. Lukashev and M. K. Shchukin flying La-11s of the 88th GIAP in the vicinity

S. A. Bakhayev, who claimed an RB-29 shot down on 26 December 1950, near Cape Seisyur (located at the mouth of the Tumen River, on the border with North Korea). The best quasi-confirmation for his claim is that an RB-29 might have been damaged on that day, but no confirmation is available. Bakhayev flew combat sorties over Korea and was awarded the prestigious Hero of the Soviet Union title and medal in 1951. (Soviet Ministry of Defence)

of Cape Ostrovnoy, some 7 to 8 nautical miles from the shore (it crashed about 18 miles out to sea). American search and rescue efforts were conducted until 9 November 1950 but they proved unsuccessful. Decades later, it briefly seemed that some of the USN fliers might have survived: according to the testimony of a certain Vladimir Trotsenko, while he was in a military hospital in the town of Novosysoyevka in the Soviet Far East, he saw four American servicemen who were being treated for injuries. He also stated that he had been shown a grave in the hospital cemetery in which a fifth American was buried. Despite the fact that Mr Trostenko's testimonies to the USRJC provided a number of accurate and seemingly credible details, an investigation at the site failed to uncover the remains of an American and in addition, archived records indicated that Mr Trotsenko was a patient in the hospital from March through to May 1951 – that is, several months before the incident in question took place.[10] Arguably, the above is an almost classic example of claims that seemed credible initially, raising high hopes that a missing piece of a Cold War history puzzle had been found and could be used to give a more complete picture of those happenings, but which disappointingly turned out to be nought. As things stand, it can be assumed that all of the ten-man crew of P2V Neptune BuNo 124283 lost their lives on 6 November 1951 when their aircraft was shot down. The men were: LTJG Judd C. Hodgson, LTJG Sam Rosenfeld, ENS Donald E. Smith, A01 Reuben Baggett, AD1 Paul Foster, ATI Erwin Raglin, AL2 Paul G. Juric, AT2 William S. Meyer, AL2 Ralph A. Wiger Jr., and AD3 Jack Lively.

Another Loss, Another Controversy

Another confirmed American loss to the interceptors of the PVO occurred on 13 June 1952, when a USAF RB-29 Superfortress (44-61810) of the 91st Strategic Reconnaissance Squadron based in Yokota, Japan, was shot down by Soviet fighters over the Sea of Japan while on a classified surveillance mission of shipping activity.[11] The US aircraft was intercepted somewhere between Ovsyankin Cape and Valentin Bay, about nine miles off the Soviet coast, by two MiG-15 fighters flown by Captain Oleg Piotrovich Fedotov and Senior Lieutenant Ivan Petrovich Proskurin. The description of what supposedly happened next was an almost exact repetition of how previous incidents were portrayed by the Soviets: the RB-29

An RB-29A of the 91st Strategic Reconnaissance Squadron, underway over Korea, showing most of the details typical of this version, and markings of that unit, to advantage. Like several other examples, this aircraft – serial 44-61727 – was also shot down by Soviet interceptors, apparently MiG-15s, while underway over the north-eastern People's Republic of China on 4 July 1952. Eleven of the crew of 13 were captured, while two died. (US DoD)

allegedly fired on the MiGs, whereupon the latter replied in kind and as a result the US aircraft burst into flames and crashed into the sea at a distance of about 18 miles from the Soviet coastline. Unfortunately, no better description of what took place is available, but in any case the bottom line is that RB-29 Superfortress (44-61810) was shot down by MiGs. Soviet aggressiveness vis-à-vis American aircraft conducting shipping surveillance missions was not accidental. A few days later, on 16 June 1952, Soviet Foreign Minister Andrey Vyshinskiy and Soviet Navy commander Admiral Nikolay Kuzniecov drew up a short memo pointing to intensive activity of US aircraft which frequently overflew Soviet ships in the Far East.[12] This memo does not mention it, yet it is likely that action to disrupt American efforts could have already been undertaken. Admiral Kuzniecov apparently reported the incident to Stalin in a separate document.[13] While Soviet radio traffic was monitored, COMINT intercepts of the incident were sparse and recognised for what they were only after the incident.[14] The sole trace of the RB-29 was some wreckage sighted about 75 miles from the Soviet coast, as well as an empty life raft, but of course material remains were of secondary importance, for the crucial question was of the fate of the crew. There was considerable, even if circumstantial, evidence that at least one man – possibly more – survived the shootdown and was held by the Soviets. Information gained from a related incident indicates that captured members of the crew of a B-29 shot down on 4 July 1952 over North Korea were interrogated in North Korea and China and were specifically asked about Major Busch, the aircraft commander of the RB-29 shot down on 13 June 1952.[15] Furthermore, Radio Moscow supposedly stated on 16 June that one unnamed survivor had been picked up by a Soviet vessel, but this broadcast could not be confirmed.[16] Moreover, the memories of a Soviet émigré to Israel, Mr Benjamin Dodin, who had the dubious 'pleasure' of being held in Soviet prison camps, implied that between four and 10 crewmen of the ill-fated RB-29 survived the crash with Busch (misspelled Bush) and Moore being mentioned by name.[17] Unfortunately, efforts to find solid evidence confirming all these reports proved unsuccessful. Considering the above, one is left with few options but to assume that Major Samuel N. Busch, Captain James A. Sculley, Captain Samuel D. Service, Captain Robert J. McDonnell, Staff Sergeant Roscoe G. Becker, SSGT Eddie R. Berg, SSGT Leon F. Bonura, MSGT William R. Homer, SSGT William A. Blizzard, SSGT Miguel W. Monserrat, AIC Danny Pillsbury and MSGT David L. Moore who constituted the crew of RB-29 (44-61810) perished when their aircraft was shot down.

Let's Get the Hell Out of Here

A few months later, on 7 October 1952, yet another RB-29 conducting a reconnaissance mission fell victim to Soviet fighters.[18] According to a memo drawn up by Marshals of the Soviet Union Aleksandr Vasilevsky and Vasily Sokolovsky, this aircraft was shot down in the vicinity of Yuri Island in the Kuriles after it allegedly repeatedly violated Soviet airspace and opened fire on intercepting Soviet aircraft.[19] The ill-fated RB-29 (44-61815) of the 91st Strategic Reconnaissance Squadron took off from Yokota in Japan and was detected by a Soviet air surveillance radar as it approached the USSR's airspace. In response, two La-11 fighters of the 368th IAP piloted by Senior Lieutenant Zhiryakov and Senior Lieutenant Lesnov were scrambled from Yuzhno-Kurilsk airfield.[20] Once the Soviets had intercepted the RB-29, they gave it warning signs and tried to force it to land but were ignored. Since their signalling failed to have the desired effect, the Soviets fired upon the US aircraft. As a result of the Soviet fighters' attack, the RB-29 suffered a catastrophic explosion with its wings separating from the fuselage and the wreckage crashing into the sea. The demise of the US aircraft was of such a violent nature that no crewman could have survived it.[21] It appears that the US airmen consciously took considerable risk, for about 20 minutes before the Soviet fighters' attack the American radar station at Nemuro warned the RB-29 crew of the presence of another aircraft.[22] The warning was acknowledged and soon thereafter the men aboard the RB-29 reported the sighting of unidentified aircraft but nevertheless decided to remain in the area. Not long after that a dramatic transmission was received from the RB-29: 'Mayday! Let's get the hell out of here!' which was the last thing heard from the aircraft and its crew.[23] Obviously a calamity befell the US aircraft: even before the RB-29's demise, USAF F-84 fighters were dispatched from Japan to assist it while a search and rescue effort commenced soon thereafter. However, this was to no avail. Hampered by bad weather, the Americans failed to find anything, not even material remains of the shot-down aircraft much less any survivors. The fashion in which the RB-29 was destroyed practically excluded anyone surviving and subsequent reports of two parachutes being sighted were dismissed as erroneous.[24] The Soviets, aided by the fact that the RB-29 went down close to shores under their control, were somewhat more successful in their recovery efforts. A patrol vessel pulled from the water a headless body in a flight suit with the name Dunkkhen Dzhon Robertson and service number 2073A.[25] The incident resulted in a Soviet protest and US counterclaims with the Americans demanding 1.6 million USD for the loss of the aircraft and its crew as well as raising the issue of sovereignty over the Kuriles and nearby islands. But all that meant little to the men who lost their lives: Captain Eugene M. English, Captain John R. Dunham, First Lieutenant Paul E. Brock, SSGT Samuel A. Colgan, SSGT John A Hirsch, A2C Fred G. Kendrick, A2C Frank E. Neail III and A1C Thomas G. Shipp. An epilogue to this tragic story was written four decades later when Captain Dunham's body, which was buried by the Soviets on Yuri Island, was exhumed, positively identified and repatriated to the USA. Last but not least, Mr Vasili Saiko, who as a young man serving on a Soviet patrol vessel pulled Captain Dunham's body from the water and took his Naval Academy ring, returned this ring via the USRJC.[26]

Axed Over Askold

The next victim of Soviet fighters was a USAF RB-50 (47-145A) shot down on 29 July 1953[27] of the 343rd Strategic Reconnaissance Squadron which flew a VHF intercept mission from Yokota in Japan.[28] According to a report subsequently filed by the Soviet Navy's commander Admiral Kuzniecov,[29] the US aircraft was tracked by Soviet radars and since it flew over their territorial waters, fighter aircraft were dispatched in response. Soviet fighters intercepted the aircraft in the vicinity of Askold Island, which they could visually make out had US markings. The US aircraft opened fire, damaging one of the Soviet fighters, whereupon the latter replied in kind, shooting it down. This rather dry account merits a few more details which can be ascertained from a number of other sources.[30] The Soviet fighters, which were MiG-17s rather than MiG-15s as misidentified in some reports, of the 88th GIAP, [31] were flown by Captain A. D. Rybakov and Senior Lieutenant Yu. M. Yablonovsky. While it is impossible to determine who fired the first shot – naturally the Americans blame the Soviets – in any case an exchange of fire took place with Captain Rybakov's MiG suffering damage to one of its wings and the fuselage. Yet the combined firepower of the MiGs' 23mm and 37mm cannons prevailed over the .50 calibre machine guns of the Boeing, first disabling its number one engine and then

The B-50 was an improved variant of the B-29, including more powerful engines, reinforced structure, and a taller fin. There were three reconnaissance variants: 14 were converted to RB-50E (photo reconnaissance), 14 to RB-50F (equipped with SHORAN radar), and 15 to RB-50G (ELINT). (US DoD)

Three Soviet-flown MiG-15 interceptors seen about to enter a firing position behind a USAF B-29, nicknamed 'Command Decision' (the bomber survived this encounter). While taken during the Korean War, this gives a fairly accurate idea of how MiG attacks looked from the perspective of the crew of US reconnaissance aircraft of this era. (USAF)

setting the number four engine on fire. Having suffered crippling damage, the RB-50 went down, crashing into the sea. The Soviet fighters flew back to Nikolaevka airfield and for this action Captain Rybakov was at a later date awarded the Order of the Red Banner and Senior Lieutenant Yablonovsky the Red Star Order. Meanwhile the Americans mounted a substantial search and rescue effort lasting until 31 July. Some crewmen managed to bail out from the stricken RB-50 before it crashed. A number of American aircraft and naval vessels, as well as a single Australian ship, searched for these survivors, of whom several sightings were made. No effort was spared; even the Soviet fishing trawler No. 423 was stopped to solicit information about possible survivors but to little effect. Regrettably, due to a number of factors such as adverse weather, in the end only co-pilot Captain John E. Roche was rescued by the USN destroyer USS *Picking* (DD685) while the bodies of two crew members, Captain Stanley O'Kelley and Master Sergeant Francis Brown, were later recovered along the coast of Japan. Captain Roche saw another crewmember, First Lieutenant James Keith, disappear beneath the surface of the sea.[32] No other survivors or bodies were found and thus a presumptive finding of death was issued by the Air Force on 14 November 1953 for the remainder of the ill-fated RB-50's crew. This hardly closed the matter since 13 out of 17 crewmen remained physically unaccounted for: Major Francisco Tejeda, Captain Robert Stalanker, Captain John Ward, Captain Edmund J. Czyz, Captain Lloyd Wiggins, Captain Frank

Beyer, Captain Warren Sanderson, SSG Donald W. Gabree, SSG Donald G. Hill, A1C Roland Goulet, A2C Earl W. Radlein Jr., A2C Charles J. Russell and A2C James E. Woods. Further efforts to establish their fate seemed imperative. Unfortunately, despite having considerable amount of recorded COMINT and other electronic data, the Americans struggled with interpreting it and putting together a cohesive picture of events.[33] For obvious reasons the Soviets were not forthcoming with information regarding the incident. Yet nothing is forever and with the end of the Cold War and the establishment of the USRJC there was renewed hope that new facts regarding the fate of the RB-50's missing crewmembers might be uncovered. Initially it seemed so, for a Russian pensioner Georgiy Yakovlevich Kravchenko, who served as an anti-aircraft gunner on Russkiy Island near Vladivostok in 1953, stated that he witnessed the shootdown of the RB-50 from his vantage point on that island.[34] He supposedly observed seven parachutes descending from the burning aircraft. In addition, another seemingly valuable witness came forward, Professor Gavril Ivanovich Korotkov, who was a former Soviet military intelligence officer. Stationed in Khabarovsk during the period of the Korean War, he claimed to have personally interrogated an American prisoner during the war. When the armistice ending the Korean War was signed, he was in Posyet, a town located not far from Vladivostok. He heard that a large US aircraft had been shot down and had crashed into the sea. In addition, he also heard that some crew members had parachuted from that aircraft. Consequently, Korotkov expected that he and other intelligence officers would be given the opportunity to interrogate the Americans. However, he and his colleagues were supposedly told that since the war was over, the Americans were not prisoners of war but spies, and intelligence officers were forbidden to meet them as they would be handled by the security services. Yet these seemingly very promising revelations failed to result in any new facts or evidence being uncovered as to the fate of the missing crewmen. For all that is known, they lost their lives when their aircraft was shot down or shortly thereafter. Unless some new and credible evidence emerges anything else falls into the category of unproven claims and speculations. Last but not least, it is worth mentioning that two days before the demise of the USAF RB-50 (47-145A), on 27 July 1953, a Soviet Il-12 military transport ferrying personnel from Port Arthur to Vladivostok was shot down in Chinese airspace by American fighters. The shootdown resulted in the death of 21 passengers and crewmen who were aboard the Ilyushin. It might have appeared that the subsequent downing of the US aircraft was deliberate revenge for the prior shooting down of the Soviet transport. Yet as attractive as such a hypothesis might be, there is no evidence backing this assertion. Hence, in view of the facts which can be established, the shootdown of the RB-50 on 29 July 1953 was solely due to the Soviets reacting to a real or perceived violation of their airspace.

The Korean War resulted in an increase in American aerial reconnaissance activities with a matching increase in Soviet air defence efforts which combined produced a string of shootdowns. However, reconnaissance aircraft being downed were not the only incidents taking place at that time in the Soviet Far East.

6
RODINA UNDER ATTACK

The Korean War also led to a rare case of a direct attack by US aircraft against Soviet territory as well as a number of incidents involving American fighters, which in the Soviet view presented a different threat of a more immediate nature than reconnaissance flights.

The Dry River Debacle

During the Second World War, the United States and the Soviet Union were allied against Germany and subsequently also against Japan. For well-known reasons this changed post-war, but during the war years this relationship resulted in the United Sates delivering substantial amounts of war material to the Soviet Union, including P-39 Aircobra and P-63 Kingcobra fighter aircraft. One of the Soviet units equipped with the latter was the 821st IAP, which fate had it was deployed for an exercise at a Far Eastern airfield named Sukhaya Rechka (the name means 'dry river'). On 8 October 1950, this location was strafed by two USAF fighter aircraft, an event most unusual even at the height of the Cold War. According to a memo drawn up by the Soviet Defence Minister, Marshal of the Soviet Union Aleksandr Vasilevsky, and the Chief of the Soviet General Staff, General Sergei Shtemenko, the airfield was attacked by two American F-80 fighters.[1] This document stated that one P-63 fighter was destroyed and went up in flames, and six more were damaged, but there were no casualties; at least none were reported. It was also claimed that after just three minutes, a flight of Kingcobras took to the air and gave chase to the attackers but to no avail. In a rather embarrassing display of ignorance about aircraft of their potentially main adversary, the Soviets speculated that the F-80s could have taken off from an aircraft carrier while in fact this US aircraft type was land-based. It also needs to be added that there is a high probability of casualties having been suffered by the Soviets in the course of the events described, for the directory of local monuments, among others, lists one monument devoted to men who lost their lives fending off an American air attack.[2] Unfortunately, the aforementioned monument seems to be missing a plaque, making it impossible to identify any potential victims. Unsurprisingly, this incident also had rather unpleasant consequences for the 821st IAP's commanding officer Colonel V. I. Savelyev and his deputy, Lieutenant Colonel N. S. Vinogradov.[3] When the Americans struck, Savelyev was attending a staff meeting while the latter was present at the airfield and ordered pilots who were in their aircraft to immediately vacate them, which somewhat negates the notion that they swiftly took to the air to give chase after the attackers. In any case, both officers were court-martialled and demoted.

As it subsequently transpired, the attack was the result of an awkward yet not impossible mistake. On 8 October 1950, four USAF pilots – First Lieutenant Norvin Evans, Jr., First Lieutenant Alton H. Quanbeck, First Lieutenant Allen J. Diefendorf, and Second Lieutenant Billy B. Watson – flying F-80 fighters of the 49th Fighter Bomber Group operating from Taegu (Daegu) airfield in South Korea were ordered to attack Chongjin airfield in the north of the country.[4] However, their numbers were soon halved: Second Lieutenant Watson failed to take off because of engine trouble

Within the frame of the Lend-Lease Program of the Second World War, the USA delivered immense amounts of war material to the USSR. Amongst other items, this included the Bell P-39 Aircobra, as shown in this photograph, and P-63 Kingcobra fighters. Ironically, on 8 October 1950 several of the latter were destroyed at Sukhaya Rechka AB by Lockheed P-80 Shooting Star fighters of the USAF, an attack that resulted from an awkward, but logical mistake. (Soviet Ministry of Defence)

while First Lieutenant Evans was forced to turn back for the same reason. Despite cloud cover and worsening weather, the remaining duo continued on to their assigned target, or so they believed. Thinking they had reached the vicinity of the target, the Americans broke through the clouds, sighting an airfield. On the ground they could see aircraft which they misidentified as P-39 Aircobras (due to the overall similarity with the P-63 Kingcobra, this is hardly a surprising mistake) and conducted repeated strafing runs. Finally, the Americans realised that the terrain did not match how it should have looked according to their pre-flight briefing, broke off the attack, and returned to base. Their target was obviously Sukhaya Rechka airfield. Unsurprisingly, the Soviets protested the attack and the Americans, not wanting to escalate the Korean War – which at that time seemed to be almost won – into a direct confrontation with the USSR, unleashed punitive measures upon those guilty. Both First Lieutenant Quanbeck and First Lieutenant Diefendorf were court-martialled: fortunately for them the court martial refused to hand down a conviction. Their commanding officer Colonel Stanton T. Smith was relived – but had somewhat of a soft landing, being brought to Seoul to direct combat operations of the Fifth Air Force.

Mauling the MiGs

The climax of the 1986 action drama 'Top Gun' depicts USN carrier-born fighters being engaged by Soviet MiGs. In the resulting aerial

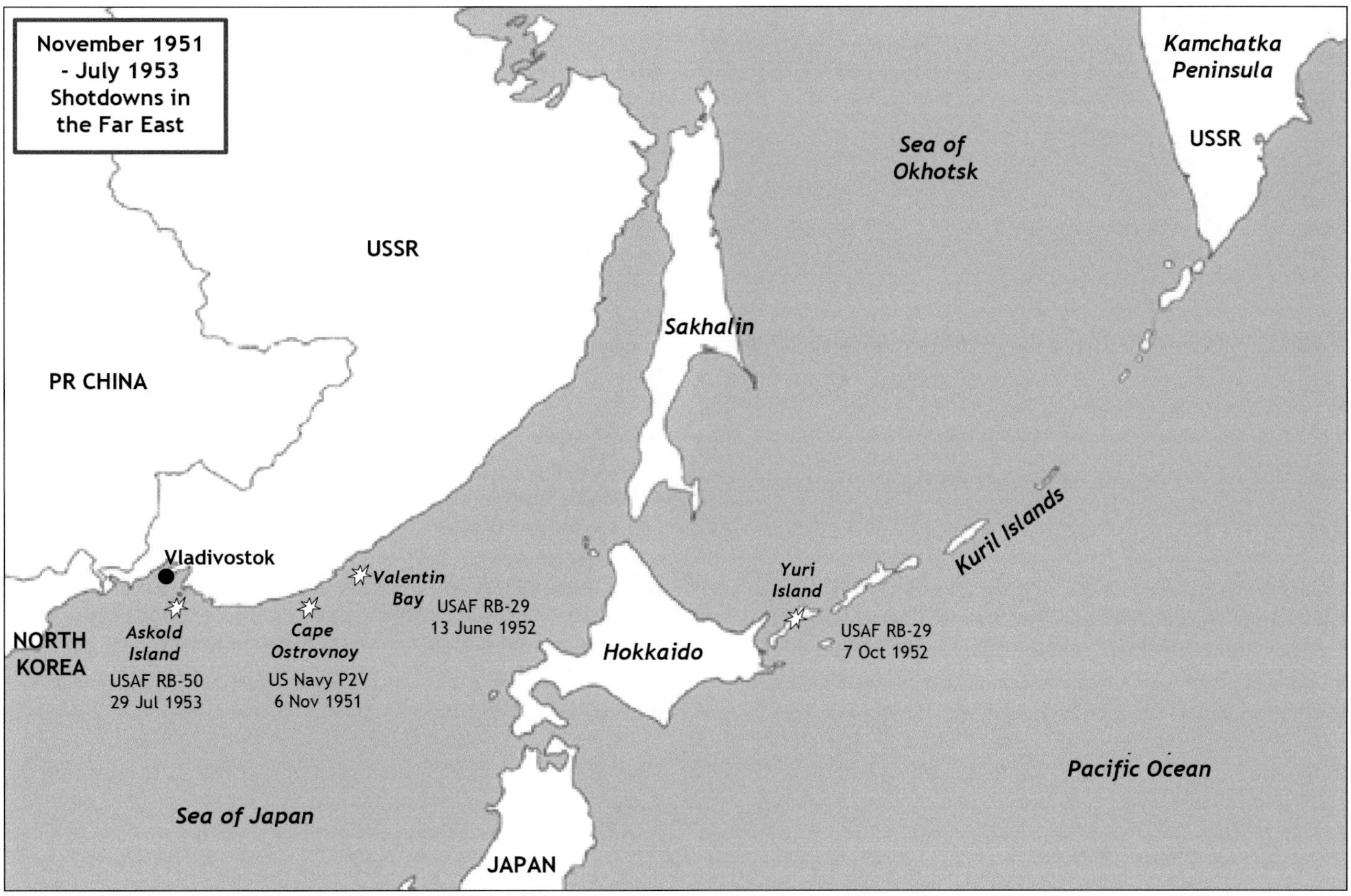

A map of the area between the Soviet Far East (Vladivostok), northern Japan, and the Pacific Ocean, where the PVO shot down four US reconnaissance aircraft between November 1951 and July 1953. Notably, Sukhaya Rechka AB was approximately one third of the distance between Vladivostok and the border with North Korea, while Yuri Island was territory of Japan that was occupied by the Soviets near the end of the Second World War (just like the southern portion of Sakhalin Island) and subsequently kept under military administration. (Map by Tom Cooper)

The Grumman F9F Panther was the first successful US carrier-borne jet fighter and served in a large number of Navy and Marine squadrons. Although its performance was somewhat inferior to that of the MiG-15, it could, and it did hold its own against PVO fighters, on 18 November 1952. Shown here is the first operational variant, the F9F-2. (US Navy)

Lieutenant (Junior Grade) Royce Williams after his victorious battle with PVO MiGs. As evident, his Panther was damaged by the MiGs' cannon shells which produced numerous fragments – the latter accounted for most of the 263 holes found in the USN aircraft after the engagement. (USN)

battle the Americans lose one of their aircraft but inflict far heavier losses upon their adversaries. Few realise that such an incident did in fact take place during the Cold War. The events about to be described took place on 18 November 1952, at a time when the Korean War was raging, and in the course of which Soviet and US airmen fought each other. However, this particular incident, despite taking place in the Far East, was not a part of that struggle due to having taken place not over the Korean Peninsula but over the neutral waters of the Sea of Japan. Moreover, the Soviet aircraft which confronted the Americans were not a part of the force deployed to fight in Korea, being instead scrambled from a Soviet airbase to counter a possible violation of Soviet airspace. For these reasons, in the author's opinion it should be considered not an episode of the Korean War but can be justifiably seen as another 'hot' incident of the Cold War.

According to the Soviets, at 1417 hours, a formation of unidentified aircraft was detected south of Cape Gamov. Subsequently, it was determined that this formation was heading towards Soviet airspace and in response four MiG-15 fighters of the 781st IAP were scrambled from Unashi aerodrome, the aircraft being flown by Captain N.M. Belyakov, Senior Lieutenant B.V. Pushkarev, Senior Lieutenant A.I. Vandayev and Senior Lieutenant V.I. Pakhomkin. When Soviet fighters encountered the US aircraft at an altitude of 6,000 metres, the US aircraft attacked, with combat commencing at 1448 hours.[5] As usual in such cases, the American version differs; on the afternoon of 18 November 1952, four F9 Panther fighters from the carrier USS *Oriskany* (CVA-34) were on a routine combat air patrol over Task Force 77 when they were vectored to intercept reportedly as many as seven MiG-15 fighters detected by radar, though there is no corroborating evidence there were any more than four in the air.[6] It would seem the opponents were evenly matched but for the MiGs' superior performance vis-à-vis the Panther. The US formation was flown by division leader Lieutenant Claire Elwood and wingman Lieutenant (Junior Grade) John Middleton as well as section leader Lieutenant Royce Williams and wingman Lieutenant (Junior Grade) David Rowlands.[7] However, soon this number was halved as Lieutenant Elwood had to return to the carrier because of a fuel pump problem, being escorted by his wingman. The two remaining USN fighters were attacked by the Soviets with combat being initiated at an altitude of about 26,000 feet, that is, close to 7,000 metres. Lieutenant Williams pulled into a hard climbing left turn and came around on the tail of one of the MiGs. He fired a burst and the Soviet fighter went down trailing smoke. Unfortunately, Lieutenant Rowlands followed the stricken MiG leaving his leader alone. Subsequently, Lieutenant Williams singlehandedly fought the remaining MiGs, vigorously manoeuvring to avoid their attacks and firing whenever an opportunity for a shot presented itself. Doing so, he fired off all 760 rounds of 20mm ammunition he had aboard and claimed no fewer than three 'kills', thus bringing his claimed score to four in total. Meanwhile Lieutenant Middleton, who had escorted away Lieutenant Elwood, returned at the end of the fight, being vectored toward a descending MiG. As he approached it, he fired a burst out of range and the pilot ejected, though this action sufficed to credit him with a single kill. In addition, Lieutenant Williams' wingman, Lieutenant Rowlands, who never fired a shot in the entire combat, was awarded a probable.

The aerial confrontation with the Soviets ended but the story was far from over. In the course of the engagement, Lieutenant

A pair of MiG-15bis in a tight formation. Note their three-digit 'Bort' numbers, as usual in the late 1940s and early 1950s, and red stars without the white outline. As during the Korean War, PVO pilots involved in the clash with USN Panthers on 18 November 1952 performed inadequately when confronted with enemy fighters. (Albert Grandolini Collection)

Williams' aircraft was severely damaged, being barely flyable, but the American pilot choose to land it on the carrier since ejecting into the cold waters of the Sea of Japan meant almost certain death from hypothermia. Flying back to USS *Oriskany* was not without hazards, for he was mistakenly fired at by escorting destroyers: fortunately, the gunners' aim matched their aircraft recognition skills and they missed. Once aboard the carrier, no fewer than 263 holes were counted in Lieutenant Williams' Panther, though most of these were from shrapnel as the 23mm and 37mm shells fired by Soviet fighters were of the explosive type producing numerous fragments when hitting a target. The aircraft – F9F-5 Panther, BuNo 125459 – was damaged beyond economic repair and thus was pushed over the side into the sea, but not before it was stripped of all useable parts. As for Lieutenant Williams, he was specifically instructed not to reveal the incident he had taken part in, which he kept in his confidence for decades, until after the demise of the Soviet Union when the Russians acknowledged it. Meanwhile, the matter was also put straight on the US side with Royce Williams being officially credited with four air to air victories and awarded the Silver Star for this action (efforts to award him the Congressional Medal of Honour were not successful). That said, a few details need to be pointed out; according to Russians sources, out of the four MiGs, three were lost with their pilots but the one flown by Senior Lieutenant B.V. Pushkarev returned to base. In addition, a number of Russian sources assert that one of the Soviet aircraft was subsequently found in shallow water close to the shore near Cape Lva with no sign of battle damage and the pilot still strapped in the cockpit.[8] Apparently, Senior Lieutenant Pakhomkin's MiG suffered from engine failure, and he lost his life trying to nurse it home. Yet even with 'only' two kills confirmed beyond any doubt, the American pilot's achievement still remains a worthy feat. Senior Lieutenant Pushkarev cheated death on this occasion but could not escape his destiny – he was deployed to China flying combat missions over Korea and was killed in action there on 5 June 1953.[9] A Panther wearing the same paint scheme as Lieutenant Williams' aircraft is displayed aboard USS *Midway* Museum in San Diego, California.

The engagement described above was not the only case – excluding the Korean War – when Soviet and American fighter aircraft battled each other. Russian sources claim that earlier, in May 1950 (unfortunately the exact date remains unknown) Soviet La-11 and US P-51 fighters clashed over the Chukotka Peninsula.[10] As a result, one of the Lavochkins was damaged but a Mustang was supposedly shot down by Captain V. S. Efremov. Unfortunately, little information beyond this is available, warranting a healthy dose of scepticism but also hope, slim as it may be, that in due time more will be revealed. In addition, Captain Vladimir Lesnov (promoted in the meantime from Senior Lieutenant) who shot down the RB-29 (44-61815) on 7 October 1952 (see above) was also reportedly involved in an incident with two USAF F-84 Thunderjets on 16 February 1953.[11] Soviet fighters confronted US aircraft which were claimed to have penetrated two kilometres deep over the territory of the USSR. In the course of the resulting engagement, Captain Lesnov was said to have shot down one of the US fighters even though his aircraft was damaged, sustaining seven hits. As with the May 1950 incident, this claim would greatly benefit from the disclosure of additional information to definitely confirm or dismiss it.

7
BALTIC BATTLES

Cold War aerial incidents were taking place not just in the Far East but also elsewhere along the Soviet Union's periphery. Reportedly a US Navy P4M Mercator reconnaissance aircraft was unsuccessfully attacked by Soviet fighters over the Baltic on 23 January 1952.[1] In addition, not only American aircraft were involved in such incidents but also ones of a nation which was ostensibly neutral, namely Sweden. For a number of historical reasons, Sweden maintained a neutral international position stretching back to the nineteenth century. The country managed to stay out of both world wars and at least officially remained neutral during the Cold War. It was understood that Sweden had a somewhat Western tilt, yet not one which would seriously compromise its proclaimed neutrality – or so it was believed by many. However, in practice, Sweden developed much closer ties with NATO generally, and the United States in particular, than was publicly admitted in those times. Suffice it to say, Sweden was deeply involved in intelligence-gathering operations which were conducted not only for its own benefit but also for NATO and US benefit.

Two Aircraft in Three Days

Swedish intelligence-gathering activities were, among others, carried out by the FRA (*Försvarets Radioanstalt*, the Defence Radio Establishment) which had a number of specially modified aircraft for that purpose.[2] Initially, only an old Ju-86 nicknamed 'Blondi' was available but subsequently two DC-3s were procured and fitted out for SIGINT missions. The latter duo were appropriately named 'Hugin' and 'Munin' after the Norse god Odin's two raven spies in the sky. Nominally the aircraft were part of 6 *Transportflyggruppen* (6th Transport Squadron) but that, however, was only an official cover as the missions they flew in reality had little to do with such mundane tasks as ferrying cargo.

On Friday 13 June 1952, one of the DC-3s – no. 79001 'Hugin' – took off from Bromma airfield at 0905 hours. The author is far from endorsing superstitions yet considering the aircraft's and the crew's fate it is hard not to notice that in this instance, Friday the 13th indeed proved to be unlucky. Regularly checking in via radio with flight control, the DC-3 made its way over the Baltic. The last full radio message from the aircraft was received at 1108 hours stating that all was well on-board. At that point in time the DC-3 was about 47 kilometres east of Fĺrö island. At 1125 hours the DC-3 tried to raise the Swedish radio station at Hägernäs, which replied with an acknowledgement, but no transmission from the aircraft followed; there was only ominous silence. The DC-3 was supposed to land back in Bromma at 1200 hours but failed to return. Soon it became obvious that it was never going to come back. At 1830 hours, the Swedes made an official press release stating that one of their aircraft on a navigation and radiotelegraphy training mission had gone missing over the Baltic Sea.

A search and rescue operation was swiftly organised with numerous aircraft and naval vessels taking part. An oil and fuel slick was sighted between the islands of Gotska Sandön and Fĺrö. Some flotsam, such as pieces of wood, light bulbs and so on were spotted as well, and one item was recovered.[3] Two days after the incident, the Swedish Navy destroyer *Sundsvall* picked up from the surface of the sea an uninflated life raft at position N 5834 E 2015. It was brought ashore, identified to have come from the lost DC-3, and found to contain splinters from shells of Soviet manufacture as determined by the Swedish National Laboratory of Forensic Science which examined it. That, for all practical purposes, settled the question of what happened to 'Hugin': it must have been shot down by Soviet fighters. Unfortunately, no survivors or even human remains were recovered though it was clear that everybody on board had perished. In all, there were eight fatalities including the three-men flight crew comprising Alvar Älmeberg (pilot), Gösta Blad (navigator) and Herbert Mattson (flight mechanic) as well as a five-man strong detachment of FRA personnel: Carl-Einar Jonsson, Ivar Svensson, Erik Carlsson, Bengt Book and Börje Nilsson. Except for the latter, who was a native of Malmö, all the others hailed from Stockholm.

Search and Rescue (SAR) missions were dangerous in their own right, as the crew of one of the Swedish PBY-5 Catalina flying boats performing them found out. According to the Soviets, on the morning hours of 16 June 1952, a Swedish aircraft, PBY-5 (47002), violated the USSR's airspace overflying the island of Hiiumaa (Dagö).[4] It was intercepted by two MiG-15 fighters of the 483rd IAP flown by Lieutenant Nikolay Semernikov and Lieutenant Ilya Yatsenko-Kosenko (leader and wingman respectively). The Soviet pilots were ordered by ground control to shoot the Swedish aircraft down, whereupon they performed repeated firing passes raking the unarmed Catalina with cannon fire. As a result, the Swedish aircraft was hit a number of times and two of its crewmen suffered wounds. The Catalina's pilot, Karl Arbin, managed to land the stricken aircraft on the surface of the sea. Because of the damage sustained, it was taking on water and soon foundered but not before the entire seven-man crew took to inflatable life rafts. Fortunately, all were swiftly rescued by the West German merchantman *Münsterland* which happened to be steaming in the vicinity. Rather unsurprisingly, the downing of an unarmed SAR aircraft generated considerable hostility towards the Soviets with demonstrations in front of the USSR's embassy in Stockholm taking place.

Putting aside displays of public anger, even though they were perfectly understandable considering the circumstances, the bottom line was that in the short time span of just three days between 13 and 16 June 1952 the Swedes lost two aircraft – a SIGNIT DC-3 and a SAR PBY-5 – both shot down by Soviet MiG-15 fighters. Eight men perished with the first, but fortunately no mortal casualties resulted from the loss of the second aircraft.

Better Late Than Never

The Swedes had forensic evidence of Soviet culpability in the DC-3 loss but the whole affair was not so simple, especially since the shot-

Two thirds of the FRA's SIGINT-collector fleet in one photograph: Douglas DC-3 serial 79001 'Hugin' is visible in the foreground. It was shot down by PVO's MiGs on Friday, 13 June 1952. Visible in the background is the old Junkers Ju-86 'Blondi'. (FRA)

down aircraft was engaged in an intelligence-gathering mission clearly at odds with Sweden's proclaimed neutrality. In 1956, the Soviet leader Nikita Khrushchev admitted to Swedish Prime Minister Tage Erlander that Soviet forces had indeed shot down the DC-3, but the two agreed not to reveal the information to the public. As a result, for several decades more the aircraft remained 'missing on a training flight', a charade which was convenient for politicians but did not do justice either to the men who lost their lives nor for their surviving family members.

However, with changes in the USSR, which was about to be dissolved anyway, new Soviet admissions finally emerged regarding the whole matter. On 30 October 1991, the Prime Minister of Sweden received the Soviet ambassador who informed the head of the Swedish government that the Soviet Union was prepared to officially admit to the shooting down of the Swedish DC-3 over international waters and that this action was a serious violation of international law. Subsequently, a Swedish mission travelled to Moscow where it was able to access documents related to the matter, as well as to talk with the pilot who shot the DC-3 down. As a result, it could be established that the Soviets were aware of Swedish intelligence-gathering activity, but that the aircraft were elusive, usually operating in international airspace or otherwise remaining out of reach. Yet Colonel Fiodor Shinkarenko, Hero of the Soviet Union and a veteran of the Winter War and the Second World War, who at that time was in command of the Baltic air defences, decided to counter these missions by shooting one of the Swedish SIGINT aircraft down over international waters if need be. For this, secrecy had to be maintained limiting the number of personnel involved to the necessary minimum. Instead of the usual leader-wingman formation, only a single fighter was to perform the mission. The pilot selected was Captain Grigory Osinskiy from the 483rd IAP; being a squadron's deputy commander for political matters he was judged to be reliable enough. Since the mission could take him relatively far out over the sea, his MiG-15 fighter was fitted with external fuel tanks. Thus, everything was ready and the only thing left was to wait for a suitable opportunity. Such an opportunity presented itself on 13 June 1952 when a radar post at Ventspils in the Soviet Republic of Latvia detected and tracked the ill-fated DC-3, which for Soviet air defences became Target No. 303. The radar post provided the vectoring data for the Soviet fighter to intercept it. Captain Osinskiy attacked his prey at an approximate position N 5805 E 2012. According to him, the DC-3's left engine was hit, catching fire. Subsequently, the Swedish aircraft made a left turn and dived steeply, disappearing into the clouds below. The DC-3 crashed into the sea with the loss of all aboard. Interestingly, the Soviet pilot also claimed to have seen a parachute which may at least in part explain why the mortal remains of only half of the crew were later recovered (see below). Having carried out the task he had been ordered to perform, Captain Osinskiy flew back, landing at an airfield in the vicinity of Riga, and was later decorated with the Order of the Red Banner but with no fanfare about it.

It took almost four decades from when the incident occurred to the point its true nature was acknowledged – better late than never, as the old adage goes. Such revelations also give hope, slim as it may be, that various other incidents (not necessary Cold War related) which are still obfuscated by cover stories, denials and so on will be eventually revealed.

From the Bottom of the Sea

Once the true nature of the missing DC-3's mission was revealed, as well as the real cause of its demise, the matter of locating its wreckage was pursued. Shortly after the aircraft was lost, one of its life rafts was picked up from the surface of the sea at the position N 5834 E 2015. Taking currents and winds into account, the life raft's starting point, which would have been the position where the DC-3 crashed, was initially calculated to be N 5821 E 2011. In 1991, the Swedish Meteorological and Hydrological Institute made new calculations and arrived at the coordinates N 5824 E 2026 with a margin of 10 kilometres, that is, the crash site and resting place of the aircraft should be somewhere in a circle having a radius of 10 kilometres with a centre at the given position. Between 1992 and 1995, the Swedish Navy conducted no fewer than eight searches in total, but each proved fruitless. Since nothing could be found it was decided in 1996 not to mount any more search missions for the lost DC-3. However, the cause of finding the missing aircraft was taken up again in 1999, although slowly at first. Three years later, in 2002, the 50th anniversary commemorations of the DC-3's loss gave new impetus to those efforts, especially since a number of individuals were making sure the matter would not be forgotten – justice to the men killed, their families and historical truth demanded it. Finally, on 10 June 2003 the DC-3 79001 'Hugin' was located at the position N 5823.522 E 2017.400 some 125 metres below the water's surface.

A row of MiG-15s at an air base of the PVO in the Baltics during the early 1950s. The 'Borts' of most of these aircraft have been changed over time, and their fuselages and fins show heavy traces of wear. (Albert Grandolini Collection)

The wreckage of DC-3 79001 seen while being examined at Muskö Naval Base, near Stockholm, after it was recovered from the bottom of the Baltic Sea. (Swedish Ministry of Defence)

The aircraft's resting place was in the western part of the circle described above.

Fifty-two years on from its demise, the DC-3 was lifted from the seabed on 19 March 2004 and brought to Muskö Naval Base for examination. It was determined that the cockpit chronometer stopped at 11:28:40, which must have been the exact time of the crash. Interestingly, the remains of only four men were found and these were identified as those of Alvar Älmeberg, Gösta Blad, Herbert Mattson and Carl-Einar Jonsson. Unfortunately, nothing was found of Ivar Svensson, Erik Carlsson, Börje Nilsson and Bengt Book and consequently they are still missing. This, together with the fact that many pieces of SIGINT equipment were not recovered either, gave rise to a number of speculative theories stipulating that the Soviets might have captured some of the crewmen and possibly found the aircraft's wreckage, stripping it of what was at that time modern electronics. Such theories, while they do not prove anything, are themselves hard to disprove. It is equally possible, even likely, that some of the crewmen managed to abandon the doomed aircraft but subsequently drowned. Unless some new findings are made or previously unknown evidence surfaces, this will remain an unresolved part of an otherwise settled matter.

One has to be content that if not everything then at least a great deal has been found out about the fate of DC-3 no 79001 'Hugin' and its crew. Since 13 May 2009, its wreckage has been on display at the Swedish Air Force Museum, Linköping, where it can be viewed today. In addition, a memorial for the eight crew members who lost their lives was erected at the Galärvarvet Church in Djurgården, Stockholm.

8
INTO THE SOVIET HEARTLAND

The reconnaissance flights described thus far were ones which only shallowly penetrated Soviet airspace, if at all. As much as such flights were useful, the 'real deal' would be to gather intelligence from the Soviet Union's interior. This in turn required deep penetration missions: flying hundreds, or thousands, of kilometres deep over the USSR. Such undertakings would be high risk but also promised high rewards. These rewards were judged to be worth the risk and as a result both the Americans and British would embark on missions taking them into the Soviet heartland.

Operation Jiu Jitsu and the Siberian Overflight

Due to a number of considerations, in 1951 the USAF loaned four RB-45C Tornados (three mission aircraft and one spare) to the RAF. They were to make nightly overflights of the western USSR to obtain radarscope photographs of potential targets there.[1] A RAF Special Duty Flight was established to operate them with aircrews sent to the USA for conversion to the type. Unfortunately, one aircraft was lost in training, but this incident did not derail the undertaking which was codenamed Operation Jiu Jitsu. Once the training was completed, the Tornados, which received British markings, were based at RAF Sculthorpe. The necessary preparations were made, including cover stories in case the aircraft went down behind the Iron Curtain (fortunately a situation testing their believability never arose) and the only thing left was to wait for the go-ahead.

Eventually this was given and the mission took place during the night of 17–18 April 1952. Three RB-45Cs took off from Sculthorpe and after refuelling over friendly territory they proceeded east, penetrating deep into Soviet airspace. One flew to the Baltic states, the second went towards Moscow and the third went south of that, flying over the centre of Russia and then arcing down to the industrial complexes in the south of Ukraine. All three intruders were detected by the Soviets but despite scrambling as many as 10 MiG-15 fighters from a number of airfields, efforts to intercept them were to no avail.[2] The aircraft were able to perform their mission, exit 'red' airspace, refuel in-flight and return to base. As a result of the mission flown, high-quality intelligence material was obtained and in addition the aircrews involved made a number of observations regarding flying and navigating over the Soviet Union. All the airmen who manned the Tornados on that night mission were decorated either with an Air Force Cross or an Air Force Medal. During peacetime these medals were given for missions which, if performed in wartime, would have probably earnt the Distinguished Flying Cross.

Subsequently, the Special Duty Flight underwent additional training and was being prepared for another mission which was intended to get radarscope photos of long-range aviation bases and

An RB-45 Tornado with its 'tools' – reconnaissance cameras – sorted out for display. A trio of such aircraft in British markings made daring deep penetration missions over the USSR in 1952 and 1954. (Albert Grandolini Collection)

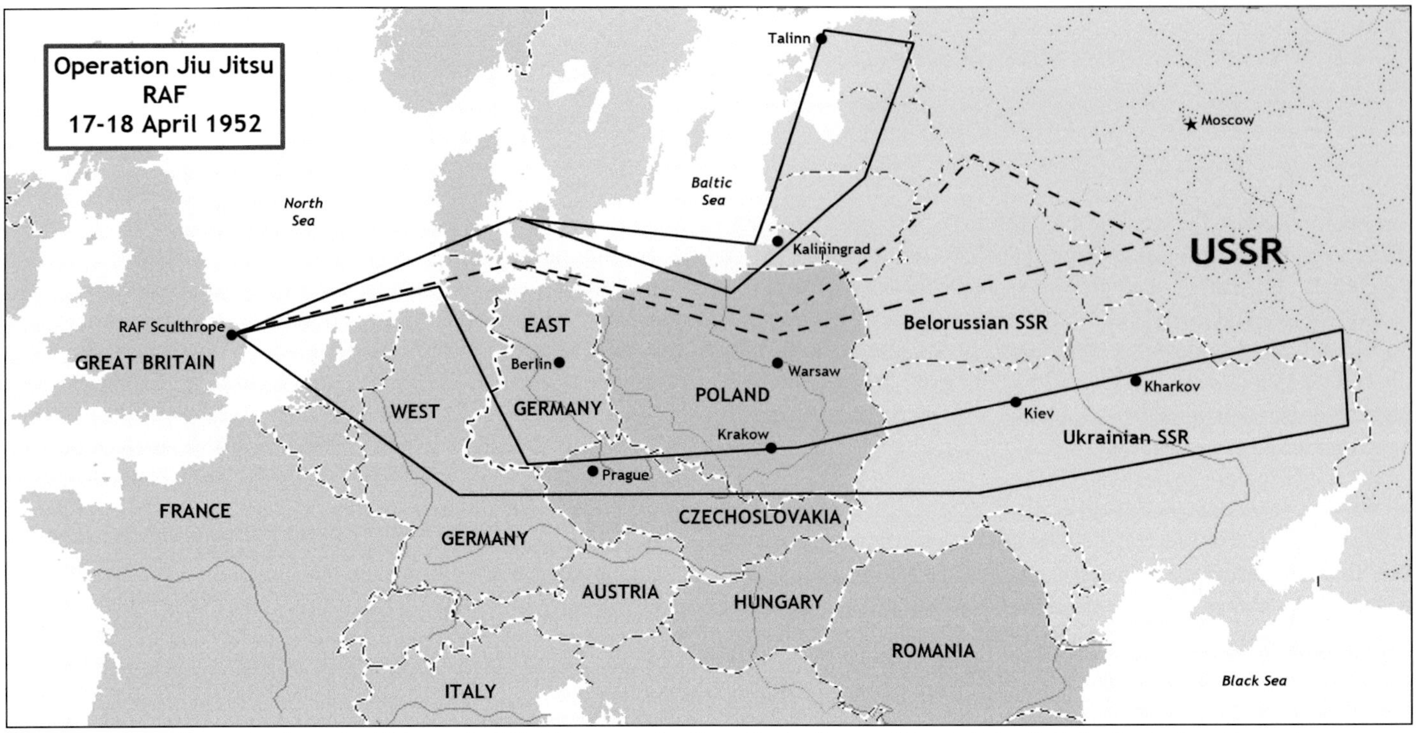

A map reconstructing routes taken by RAF-operated RB-45Cs during the Operatin Jiu Jitsu, on 17 and 18 April 1952. (Map by Tom Cooper)

other Soviet facilities. The sortie was planned for the night of 12–13 December 1952. However, only a few days before the overflight was to be made, it was not only called off, but the Special Duty Flight was disbanded. Neither British aerial reconnaissance efforts in general nor Operation Jiu Jitsu in particular were over, however.

The Americans were not far behind the British, sending a modified B-47 of the 306th Bomber Wing deep into Soviet airspace, with a second backup Stratojet circling outside of it, tasked to reconnoitre airfields in north-eastern Siberia. The flight route took the B-47s from Eielson AFB, Alaska, north to a refuelling point near Point Barrow, then west past Wrangel Island to a point near Ambarchik. Subsequently it turned southeast, to parallel the length of the Chukotskiy Peninsula to Provideniya and then east to return to Eielson. The two B-47s took off on 15 October 1952 and after in-flight refuelling, one flew into Soviet airspace while the other took up a racetrack pattern in an area over the Chukchi Sea. The mission lasted well over seven hours, covering around 3,500 miles of which 800 were over Soviet territory. As a result, camera and radar photographs of five Soviet airfields were taken.[3] Unsuccessful attempts to intercept by MiG-15 fighters were observed from the Stratojet while it was in Soviet airspace. There is little in Russian sources regarding the whole affair bar acknowledging that the overflight could not be effectively countered.

Kapustin Yar

If 1952 was the year Anglo-American deep penetrating overflights of the Soviet Union started, then 1953 was when one of the arguably most mysterious operations of this kind may have taken place. Before going into details, it needs to be pointed out that thus far, the main strategic threat to the United States and West in general came from Soviet bombers, even if due to a number of factors this threat was not immediate but rather potential.[4] This is why airfields where heavy bombers could be based were high on the list of locations to be reconnoitred. However, the Soviets were meanwhile also developing missiles, which would constitute an even greater menace. For these reasons it became imperative to gather intelligence on Soviet rocketry. Much of the latter was obtained from German scientists returning from the USSR after their tenure of forced work for the Soviets. Among other things, it was learned that at a remote location in the Astrakhan Oblast, around 100 kilometres east of Volgograd (Stalingrad) at a site known as Kapustin Yar, there was a Soviet facility for the development as well as test launching of rockets and missiles.

In view of the above, it is not surprising that Kapustin Yar was supposedly overflown by a RAF Canberra probably sometime in 1953. Reportedly it took off from Giebelstadt, in West Germany, flew over Czechoslovakia, Poland, Soviet Ukraine, eventually overflying Kapustin Yar, then turned southeast to the Caspian Sea and finally landed at an airfield in Iran. Soviet fighters made ineffective attempts at interception though they managed to get a few rounds off at the British aircraft. As a result, the Canberra was lightly damaged and suffered a slight vibration. Because of the latter, although Kapustin Yar was photographed as planned, the pictures taken were blurred and revealed little detail of the site itself. This is, in short, the most widely accepted version of the story which was critically analysed by the well-known British defence and aviation writer Chris Pocock.[5] According to him, if the flight happened at all (which is far from certain) it would have most likely taken place on 27 August 1953 and would have been performed by a RAF Canberra of 540 Squadron. However, as per that analysis, this was far from certain because files pertaining to this supposed operation are unavailable: either still being classified or possibly not existing to begin with. It may very well be that the Kapustin Yar overflight did not take place at all, being confused with Operation Jiu Jitsu, Operation Robin or some other aerial reconnaissance operation.

Should the Kapustin Yar mission have happened, it would have certainly left a trace in Soviet sources. Western researchers obtained the recollections of a Soviet pilot Lieutenant Mikhail Shulga and the Soviet airman gave an undated but vivid description of a failed attempt to intercept a foreign reconnaissance aircraft which more or less matches the supposed Kapustin Yar overflight.[6] However, Lieutenant Shulga served in the southern USSR in 1954[7] and for

The post-war Soviet air defences began their operational history flying a large number of piston-engined aircraft left over from the Second World War or pressed into service immediately after. Probably the best type in service as of the late 1940s was the Lavochkin La-11, the most powerful piston-engined fighter manufactured in the USSR. This example may have served with one of the units deployed in the Far East, before being sold to the People's Republic of China, where it served in the nascent People's Liberation Army Air Force (PLAAF) in the 1950–1951 period. (Artwork by Tom Cooper)

The Mikoyan i Gurevich MiG-15 (ASCC/NATO-codename 'Fresco') was the first successful jet fighter to enter service in the USSR with swept wings and capable of reaching high transonic speeds. Created by a design bureau specialised in developing high-altitude interceptors, it was a design custom-made to combat such bombers as the B-29, for which purpose it received heavy armament in the form of two 23mm automatic cannons with 80 rounds per gun, and one 37mm cannon with 40 rounds. While slow-firing, and having a low muzzle velocity, such weapons provided tremendous punch: the Soviets calculated that 2-3 hits from either gun would be enough to knock out a B-29. The MiG-15 was pressed into series production in late 1948, and at least 15,000 were manufactured over the following years. This example served with the 29th Guards Interceptor Aviation Regiment in the Far East, before being handed over to the PLAAF in August 1950. (Artwork by Tom Cooper)

With early MiG-15s having several deficiencies, the MiG OKB quickly developed an improved variant, the MiG-15bis, powered by the improved Klimov VK-1 engine, and equipped with larger air brakes to prevent the jet from exceeding the speed of Mach 0.92, at which control surfaces became ineffective. Series production began in 1950, and large numbers were quickly rushed into service with the Soviet air defences. Like the MiG-15, the bis was easy to maintain but not the easiest aircraft to fly. Moreover, its armament was ill-suited for air combat against high-speed and manoeuvring targets like the US-made fighter jets encountered during the Korea War – where, in 1952, this example may have been flown by Semyon Fedorets of the 689th Guards Interceptor Aviation Regiment, credited with seven aerial victories. (Artwork by Tom Cooper)

The usual method of painting MiG-15s (and all the other combat aircraft types in service with the PVO in the 1950s and 1960s) was relatively simple: after being assembled at the factory, each aircraft would receive a layer of varnish, followed by one layer of clear lacquer mixed with 10 percent aluminium powder, and then another consisting of clear lacquer mixed with 5 percent aluminium powder. With this near-transparent, highly polished colour 'mirroring' surroundings, while also showing the colour of metal surfaces on which it was applied (where darker, bluish surfaces, like air brakes, were usually made of steel, while the rest was of aluminium), it became colloquially known as 'silver grey'. By 1953, experience from the Korean War prompted the Soviets to start camouflaging their MiG-15s. Around the same time the Soviet Union accepted the British Standard 381C as the standard for its colour production. As a result, this example, which served with the Soviet air defences in the Far East in the 1953–1954 period, had its top surfaces painted in grey-green BS381C/283, and undersides in light admiralty grey BS381C/697. (Artwork by Tom Cooper)

Striving to further improve the MiG-15bis, the MiG OKB eventually designed an entirely new type, with stretched fuselage, bigger fin and thinner wing of larger surface, a rear-view mirror atop the cockpit transparency (based on experience from the Korean War), and the more powerful Klimov VK-1F engine. Designated the MiG-17 (ASCC/NATO-codename 'Fresco'), this entered production in 1952, and 5,467 were manufactured over the following years. Like the MiG-15 before, the MiG-17 was always painted in two layers of clear lacquer, mixed with 10 percent and 5 percent aluminium powder, respectively, resulting in the 'silver grey' overall appearance. By the time it entered service, the V-VS and the PVO introduced the practice of using two-digit 'Bort' numbers on their aircraft (instead of up to three at earlier times). These were usually applied in the factory, nearly always in red and outlined in black or dark blue. This example served with the 136th Interceptor Aviation Regiment as of 1955-1956. (Artwork by Tom Cooper)

In early 1953, the further improved MiG-17F entered production, which promptly proved the most-popular variant of this prolific type. The MiG-17F was powered by the VK-1F engine, with an afterburner containing convergent-divergent nozzle and fuel system, which in turn necessitated a redesign of the rear fuselage. Notably, like the MiG-15bis before, it included an IFF-antenna installed on the top of the centre fuselage. This example belonged to the 117th Interceptor Aviation Regiment, and on 2 September 1958 was piloted by Senior Lieutenant Kucheryaev, when he led the intercept of the USAF C-130A-II 60-258 – a task Kucheryaev and his wingman, followed by two other MiG-17-pilots, completed without too many troubles, thanks to the heavy armament of their jets. As usual for the time, his MiG still wore the red Bort number 17: uneven Borts were always assigned to flight-leaders. (Artwork by Tom Cooper)

Throughout their service, the mass of MiG-15s and MiG-17s served as day and fair-weather interceptors only. MiG-17F was no exception to this, but the next mass-produced variant, the MiG-17PF (ASCC/NATO-codename 'Fresco C') was equipped with the Izumrud RP-2 radar. Although still dependent on guidance from the ground, the MiG-17PF thus became capable of finalising interception by night and in poor weather – a capability that became ever more important because of the nocturnal activity of Western intelligence-gathering aircraft within Soviet airspace. By the time the MiG-17PF entered service (668 were built in total), the PVO introduced the practice of applying Borts to its aircraft in light blue, outlined in black. This example served with the 166th Guards Interceptor Aviation Regiment. (Artwork by Tom Cooper)

By the mid-1950s, the Soviets rushed their first air-to-air missiles into mass production: the RS-1U (ASCC/NATO-codename 'AA-1 Alkali'), itself a part of the Kaliningrad K-5 weapons system (still centred on the Izumrud RP-2 radar). Correspondingly, a total of 47 MiG-17PFs were re-equipped with the K-5 weapons system, including four underwing hardpoints for K-5s. (Artwork by Tom Cooper)

The first of the second generation of Soviet jet fighters, and the first supersonic interceptor to enter service with PVO was the MiG-19S, which entered production in 1955. Almost immediately, the type became involved in several intercepts of Western reconnaissance aircraft, though without much success before autumn 1957, when one of the PVO's MiG-19S pilots became the first to visually observe a U-2 over the USSR. Marred by problems caused by poor insulation between the engines and fuel tanks in the rear fuselage, and overheating of these and the hydraulics system, the MiG-19 continued soldiering and on 1 July 1960, Captain Vasyli Polyakov from the 174th Guards Interceptor Aviation Regiment shot down the RB-47H 53-4281 over the Bering Sea, killing four of the crew. While the appearance of Polyakov's MiG-19S remains unknown, this example is known to have served with 365th Interceptor Aviation Regiment based at Aivazian AB, on the Kola Peninsula, around the same time. (Artwork by Tom Cooper)

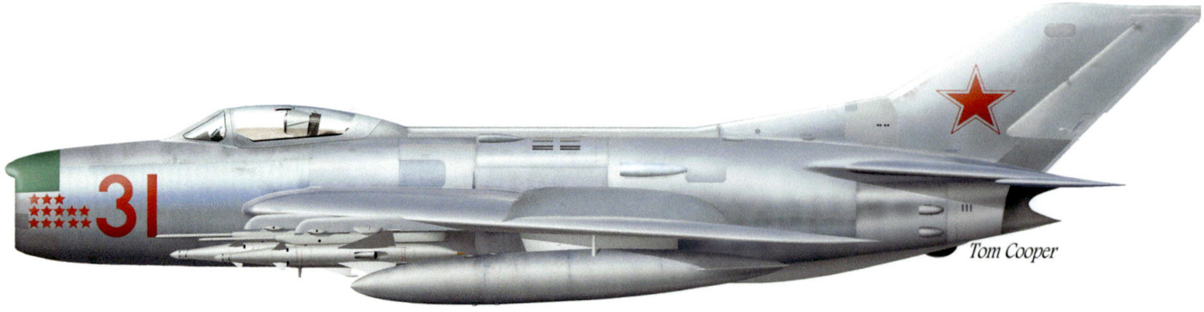

With the PVO being reorganised into a total of eight independent Air Defence Armies and two Air Defence Districts, and introducing to service large numbers of S-75 Dvina high-altitude SAM systems, MiG-19 and Su-9 interceptors at almost the same time, there was urgent need for establishment of a major training centre, where its troops could be trained for their task. Thus came into being the 116th Training Centre at Astrakhan AB, and the 18th Training Centre in Krasnovodsk AB. The 1st Squadron of the latter was equipped with MiG-17PFUs, while the 2nd received 16 MiG-19PMs. One of the latter is illustrated here, decorated with a total of 13 'kill markings' (in the form of small red stars, applied near the intake), for the number of simulated targets destroyed during different tests and training sorties. (Artwork by Tom Cooper)

Ironically, the first missile-armed interceptor in the USSR was this heavily modified Tupolev Tu-4 bomber – a copy of the US-made B-29 Superfortress – a reconstruction of which is shown here. It was equipped to carry and launch G-300 air-to-air missiles, which were scaled down versions of V-300s from the S-25 SAM system with radar beam-riding guidance. The G-300 was quickly replaced by the improved G-301, which had semi-active radar homing guidance and a range of about 35km. Despite a series of test-firings in 1952 and 1953, the project was eventually terminated a year later, when the Soviets concluded that although the system was functional, it was also impractical, and a much lighter missile would be necessary. As far as is known, the Tu-4 in question wore no other markings than the usual national insignia in six positions, and, possibly, its serial number – 226404 – on the fin. (Artwork by Tom Cooper)

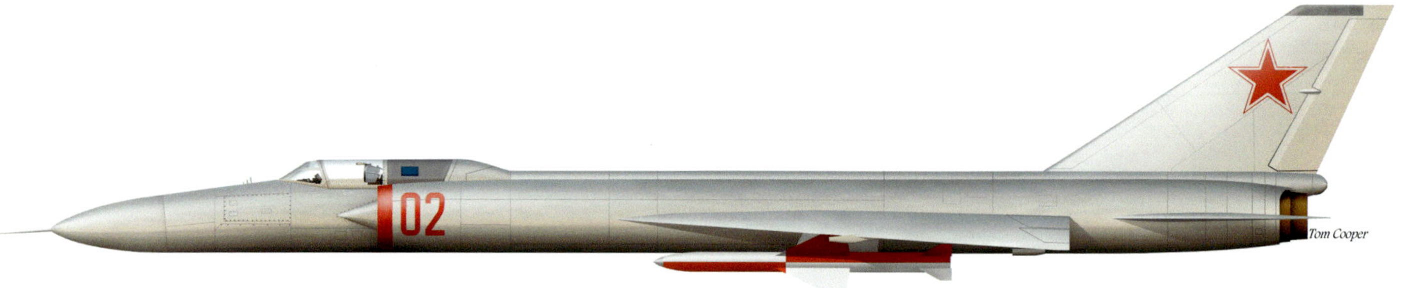

Another stillborn Soviet interceptor project was the Lavochkin La-250 Anakonda. Development started in 1953, by when it became clear that the much-expected Yakovlev Yak-25 would be too slow and unable to intercept high-altitude targets. The La-250 was expected to become capable of intercepting targets underway at 1,250km/h (780mph or Mach 1.18) at an altitude of 20,000m (66,000ft) up to 500km away from its base. The first flight took place on 16 July 1956, but the project then suffered numerous problems with its lightweight airframe, the K-15U radar and Klimov VK-9 engines, resulting in several crashes. After making only 21 flights in three years, the project – including the K-15 weapons system, mock-up missiles which are shown as in their final configuration, installed on underwing hardpoints – was cancelled in 1959. (Artwork by Tom Cooper)

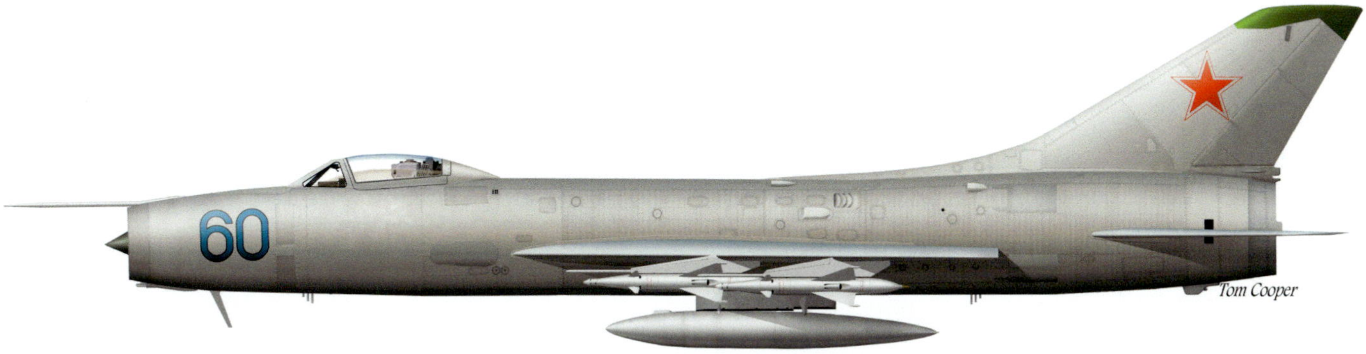

With the La-250 being plagued by development issues, and the MiG-21 – designed around exactly the same planform – proving too light and too short-ranged for the task, eventually it fell to the Sukhoi Su-9 to become the most potent high-speed/high-altitude interceptor of the PVO in the early 1960s. Its prototypes set several new records in sustained speed and altitude, while series production was initiated in 1959. In operations, the Su-9 proved capable of reaching up to Mach 2 at 20,000 metres (66,000ft) while armed with RS-2U/K-5 missiles. Unsurprisingly, one was involved in intercepting Francis Gary Powers' U-2 on 1 May 1960, but because the jet was unarmed, its pilot, Captain Igor Mentyukov, was ordered to attempt ramming. Mentyukov missed and then ran out of fuel but claimed that it was his slipstream that caused the U-2 to break apart. The Su-9 continued serving with the PVO through the 1960s, and became involved in numerous other intercept attempts, but is not known to have ever scored any aerial victories , bar a few aerostats. This example served with the 393th Guards Interceptor Aviation Regiment of the Baku Air Defence District. (Artwork by Tom Cooper)

The Yakovlev Yak-25 was a turbojet-powered interceptor, the development of which was initiated on direct order from Joseph Stalin in 1951. Once testing proved that its prototypes were exceeding all the PVO's operational requirements – except those for speed – and that it was superior to the competing Lavochkin La-200B, it entered series production in 1954 and operational service as the Yak-25M a year later, equipped with the RP-6 Sokol radar and two Nudelman NL-37 37mm automatic cannons with 50 rounds each. The type proved highly popular in service, and became involved in dozens of intercept attempts against Western aircraft, but its low maximum speed (1,090km/h or 677mph) and massive problems with the height-finding equipment of early Soviet ground-based radars made it ineffective at altitudes above 10,668m (35,000ft). This Yak-25M served with the 524th Interceptor Aviation Regiment at the Letnoerzerskiy AB (Arkhangelsk region) in the early 1960s. (Artwork by To Cooper)

The first Western aircraft ever confirmed as intercepted and shot down by the PVO during the Cold War was this US Navy Consolidated PB4Y-2 Privateer, felled by La-11 interceptors over the Baltic Sea on 8 April 1950. Assigned to Patrol Squadron 26 (VP-26), it wore the serial number 59645 and was nicknamed the 'Turbulent Turtle'. It was painted in non-specular blue overall, and its livery was badly worn out after months of intensive operations around the periphery of the USSR in the Baltic Sea. Frequently rotated between its home-base, Naval Air Station Patuxent River, and forward base, Port Lyautey in French Morocco, it wore the tailfin code HB from November 1946 until July 1950, when this was replaced by EB. While earlier photographs show it wearing a large 7 on the forward fuselage, and service title Navy on the rear, as far as is known, both had been removed by April 1950. It is shown here fully armed, though is believed to have been unarmed at the time it was shot down. (Artwork by Tom Cooper)

On 18 November 1952, at least four MiG-15s of the PVO clashed with two F9 Panthers of VF-781, flying a combat air patrol over USS *Oriskany* (CVA-34). Flying F9F-5 BuNo 125459/D106, Lieutenant Royce Williams claimed three MiGs as shot down. His wingman, Lieutenant Junior Grade David Rowlands, flew F9F-5 BuNo 126034/D109, but scored no kills, while Lieutenant Junior Grade John Middleton flew F9F-5 BuNo 126969/D114 and was credited with one kill (although, probably, scoring none). The main artwork shows Williams' F9F-5 at the time of that clash: the jet returned for a safe landing on *Oriskany* but was subsequently written off due to combat damage and dumped into the sea. Middleton's F9F-5, shown inset, thus became the only one known to have worn kill markings, even though latest research indicates that he shot down no MiGs. (Artworks by Tom Cooper)

RB-29A serial number 42-9400, nicknamed 'Tiger Lil', was one of several aircraft of this type shot down by the PVO while flying ELINT/SIGINT-intelligence-gathering mission along the periphery of the USSR. Assigned to the 6007th Composite Group of the 91st Strategic Reconnaissance Squadron, the modified bomber was intercepted by MiG-15s of the PVO and received hits into one of its wing tanks. The crew bailed out safely: the navigator, 2nd Lieutenant Sigredo Angulo, became entangled in his parachute lines and drowned in the sea, while others were recovered by a US military vessel. Tiger Lil – which wore the crest of the 15th Air Force, USAF, on its fin – remained airborne after being abandoned by her crew: the modified bomber crashed into the town of Nemuro in Japan, though fortunately causing no civilian casualties. The prominent nose art had been removed at the time of the shooting-down. (Artwork by Tom Cooper)

Sadly, there are no photographs of the RB-47H serial number 53-4281 left. This reconstruction was prepared with assistance from Robert Hopkins III, an acknowledged military aviation historian. Nicknamed 'The Little Toy Dog', this jet was assigned to the 55th Strategic Reconnaissance Wing when intercepted and shot down by a MiG-19 flown by Captain Vasyli Polyakov from the 174th Guards Interceptor Aviation Regiment, PVO, over the Bering Sea off Cape Svyatov Nos, on 1 July 1960. As of the time, The Little Toy Dog had an early version of the AN/ALD-4 ELINT-gathering system installed under Project Silver King. This included a lower number of antennas on the rear fuselage, and a large pod later installed low on the right side of the centre fuselage. Similarly, while many RB-47Hs of the 55th Strategic Reconnaissance Wing had the front doors of their undercarriage painted in red, and the 'last three' of their serial applied there in white, this was not yet the case with this example as of July 1960. (Artwork by Tom Cooper)

In 1951, the USAF provided four RB-45C Tornado reconnaissance bombers to the Royal Air Force for operations over the western USSR. Wearing the full British insignia, but no serials or other markings, three jets were deployed from RAF Sculthorpe during Operation Jiu Jitsu on 17–18 April 1952, which took them deep over the western USSR. The fourth aircraft was kept back as a spare. All three were detected by the PVO, and as many as 10 MiG-15s were scrambled to intercept, but to no avail. Encouraged, the Special Duty Flight of the RAF then prepared another mission, but this was cancelled. As far as is known, all four RB-45Cs operated by the British were left in their 'bare metal overall' livery, with anti-glare panels in dark green applied along the upper front fuselage, and top forward surfaces of engine nacelles. (Artwork by Tom Cooper)

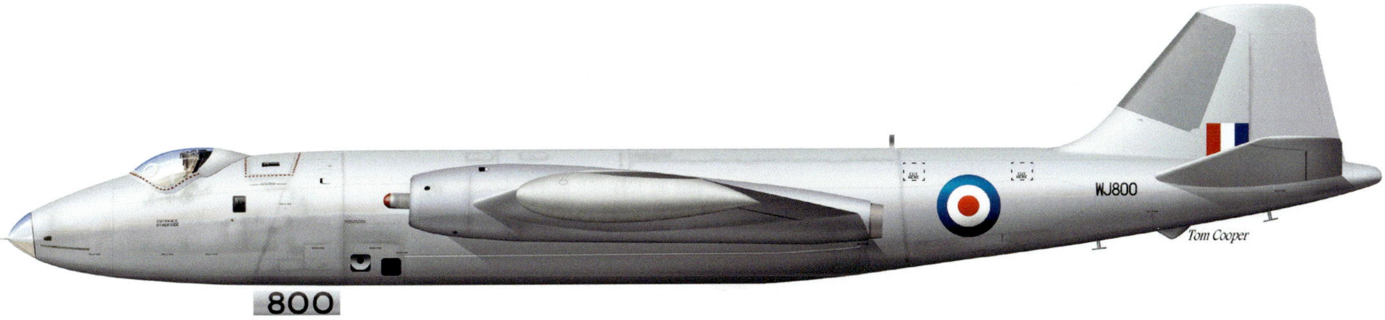

Reconnaissance variants of the famous English Electric Canberra bomber became involved in clandestine reconnaissance operations over the USSR at least as early as 1953, and through that and the following year may have reached targets as deep within the Soviet Union as Kapustin Yar. As far as is known, the Soviets launched numerous intercept attempts but all remained fruitless – which is the probable reason why so little about the operations in question is known today. The example illustrated here was a Canberra PR.Mk 7 of No. 13 Squadron, perhaps the most advanced reconnaissance aircraft in service as of 1955–1968. At the time, all the Canberras wore the high-speed silver finish overall, and their usual set of national markings and serials on the rear fuselage and the cover of the undercarriage bay. Subsequently, Canberra's US-made variant, manufactured under licence as the Martin RB-57, saw even more action, especially in the Far East. (Artwork by Tom Cooper)

Probably the most famous and most controversial operation of the PVO prior to the downing of Power's U-2 in May 1960, resulted in the intercept and shootdown of the USAF C-130A-II Hercules serial number 60-528, from the 7406th Support Squadron, over Soviet Armenia, on 2 September 1958. The aircraft – left in bare metal overall but having most of its fin and rear fuselage painted in dayglo orange, as usual at the time – launched from Incirlik AB in Turkey, for a reconnaissance mission along the border with the USSR. It carried six flight crew from the 7406th Squadron and 11 mission specialists of the 6911th Radio Group Mobile. For unknown reasons, it flew off course and into Soviet airspace, where it was intercepted and shot down by two pairs of MiG-17s from the 117th and 168th Interceptor Aviation Regiments. The burning wreckage came down about 55km northwest of Yerevan, killing all 17 crewmembers. (Artwork by Tom Cooper)

A map depicting the areas of responsibility of the PVO as around 1959–1960, when it included eight independent air defence armies (2, 4, 6, 8, 10, 11, 12, and 14) and two air defence districts. Lacking clear source of reference, the borders of areas of responsibility between armies and districts are based on those of contemporary Military Districts and other major units, and should be considered 'provisional/probable'. (Map by Tom Cooper)

Some US and British operations deep inside Soviet airspace prompted the PVO into scrambling entire formations of MiGs to intercept them. Most of the time, Western aircraft made good their escape, even if it was often a narrow one. This photograph shows a 'zveno' (four-ship) of early MiG-17s – a version recognisable by the lack of afterburner. (Albert Grandolini Collection)

this reason his recollections obviously cannot refer to an overflight which supposedly took place in 1953. Moreover, when describing the purported incident in another piece, the Russian author invoked a Western source: The Quarterly Journal of Military History Spring 1997.[8] Similarly, as far as could be ascertained, other Russian publications either fail to confirm a 1953 overflight of Kapustin Yar or if they describe such an incident the narratives resemble Western accounts so strongly, that even if no Western publication is cited it still seems that the source of the information was not Soviet but rather Western in origin.

The nature of Cold War aerial operations, especially of deep penetration overflights of the Soviet Union is such that, despite a large amount of information from Soviet and Western sources having become available, some events still cannot be definitely disproved or confirmed, with one such being the 1953 Kapustin Yar overflight. That said, taking into consideration available information and unless new disclosures are made, it appears likely that no such overflight took place in 1953. If a RAF Canberra, or other British or US aircraft, flew over Kapustin Yar or anywhere close it could have possibly happened at the earliest in 1954 though certainly such did occur later.[9]

Robin, Jiu Jitsu and Other Operations

Regardless as to whether the Kapustin Yar mission took place or not, deep penetration overflights of the Soviet Union have been frequently associated with Operation Robin, during the course of which RAF Canberras flew a number of photoreconnaissance sorties. However, if declassified information published by the United Kingdom's National Council of Aerial Photography (NCAP) is anything to go by, the missions flown by the RAF's Nos 58 and 540 Squadrons were not over the USSR.[10] Instead, they covered parts of Austria, East Germany, Hungary, Egypt, Yugoslavia, France, Israel/Palestine, Lebanon, and Syria but not the Soviet Union – with the caveat that the catalogue of these missions is incomplete. Similarly, Canberras of No. 192 Squadron flew a number of missions during Operation Reason over the Baltic, Black, and Caspian Seas during 1953–54. The flights were staged out of Bodö (Norway), Wunstorf (Germany), Luqa (Malta) and Nicosia (Cyprus).[11]

In any case, the Soviets registered a number of deep (circa 300 kilometres and occasionally more) airspace penetrations by aircraft which they identified as Canberras.[12] On the night of 4–5 January 1954, a foreign aircraft presumed to be a Canberra, possibly from the RAF's 192 Squadron, flying from the direction of Iran, penetrated Soviet airspace 360 kilometres deep over the Caspian Sea. In response, eight MiG-17 fighters were scrambled, which not only failed to intercept the intruder but one of them was lost: Lieutenant Antsiferov of the 177th GIAP crashed on take-off. The next night there was a repeated incursion and again efforts to counter it proved unsuccessful, but at least nobody crashed or suffered any other mishaps. The primary reasons for the failures were inadequate training of both pilots and ground controllers as well as limitations of the equipment available. After more than two months, the violator reappeared during the night of 24–25 March and again interception attempts were fruitless, prompting the arrival of a commission form Moscow – just in time to witness another overflight on 26–27 March and yet another failure to intercept it. This commission did not establish much except what was already known, namely that training was inadequate, and shortcomings of available equipment did not help. RAF Canberra overflights and unsuccessful Soviet attempts to intercept them are quasi-confirmed in British sources: reportedly, in the course of a mission by 193 Squadron over the Caspian Sea, the signals of a Soviet-made *Izumrud* (ASCC/NATO-codename 'Scan Odd') air intercept radar were recorded but the event is placed on an unspecified day sometime in May 1954.[13]

Since the need to collect intelligence from deep within USSR territory persisted, it prompted a repetition of Operation Jiu Jitsu. For that purpose, the RAF's Special Duty Flight was reformed with basically the same crews from the 1952 overflight, and the three RB-45Cs with British markings being again sent over the Soviet Union on the night of 28–29 April 1954. Taking off from RAF Sculthorpe, the trio was, as on the previous mission, meant to cover the Baltic, central and southern regions of the European part of the USSR. The intruders were detected, which resulted in a flurry of Soviet air defence activity. In all, no fewer than 92 fighters were scrambled but again efforts to intercept ended in complete failure.[14] There were allegations[15] that two Soviet pilots, Batyshev and possibly Sysoev were ordered to ram one of the Tornados. Indeed, Colonel Batyshev confirmed that the idea to ram an intruding aircraft was contemplated; however, at that time he served in the Baku district and this half-baked proposal was made in response to the earlier

Canberra overflights.[16] In addition to fighter aircraft, anti-aircraft artillery also went into action: an AA battery in the Minsk district fired 14 rounds while three batteries in the Kiev district fired 81 rounds (all were 100mm rounds from KS-19 guns) but they failed to hit even though some bursts were close.[17] Squadron Leader Rex Sanders cut short his mission because of the heavy and well placed AA fire he encountered, but the other Tornados completed theirs.[18] Once more, Western aircraft were able to penetrate deep into Soviet airspace and make good their escape unscathed. However, arguably the greatest Soviet air defence failure in the first half of the 1950s was yet to come.

Hitting a 'Hell Kind of a Seagull'

Nightly overflights in the early months of 1954 were undoubtedly dramatic but the climax would come in May that year. Before describing the unfolding action, a few words explaining the background which led to it seem fitting: even a cursory look at the map will show why northern Russia was a sensitive area if it ever came to an all-out confrontation between the USA and the USSR. It is therefore not surprising that the Americans, including General Curtis LeMay who headed the USAF's SAC, were keen to obtain photographic intelligence of Soviet installations, including airfields, which were located there. A mission with this purpose in mind was planned for May 1954: three RB-47s of the USAF's 91st Strategic Reconnaissance Wing were to approach Soviet airspace, with one aircraft tasked to not only penetrate it but to cover well over 1,000 kilometres of Soviet territory flying from Murmansk to Arkhangelsk, then Onega and turning southwest to escape into Finnish airspace. In particular, it was to photograph nine Soviet airfields specifically to ascertain if the new MiG-17 fighter was being deployed from them.[19] As subsequent events were to show, the Americans not only found out they were, but got to see them somewhat too close for comfort. The three RB-47Hs took off from RAF Fairford near Oxford early on 8 May 1954. Initially the mission was uneventful but after refuelling off southern Norway at a designated departure point about 100 miles north of Murmansk, two of the three aircraft turned back while the third flew on towards Soviet airspace. The crews of the two were not briefed on the third's mission as the fewer people that were in the know about such a sensitive undertaking the better, yet in what was a display of true professionalism, they did not break radio silence to inquire but silently returned to base. The third RB-47, which was crewed by Captain Harold Austin, pilot; Captain Carl Holt, co-pilot; and Major Vance Heavilin, navigator, pressed on, soon finding themselves over Soviet territory.

Meanwhile the Soviets detected not just one but two intruders.[20] The second supposedly penetrated Soviet airspace in the vicinity of Pechenga before exiting into Finland, and no attempt was made to intercept it. However, the first was clearly on a heading leading it ever deeper over the Soviet Union, becoming the focus of air defence efforts. The intruder was tracked flying at an altitude of 12,000 metres with a speed of 760–840 km/h. Captain Austin's RB-47 which maintained an altitude of 40,000 feet (12,192 metres) and 440 knots (814.88 km/h) airspeed. In order to intercept it, the Soviets scrambled no fewer than 13 MiG-17 fighters from six

Illustrative of the appearance of a Stratojet to a MiG pilot scrambled to intercept and approach it from behind and below, this photograph shows an RB-47H later during that type's career, while used as a test-rig. Note also the 'bulge' installed low in the centre fuselage instead of the usual bomb bay: this was the compartment carrying, depending on equipment, two or three 'ravens' (the operators of mission-specific equipment). (Albert Grandolini Collection)

A formation of MiG-17s of the PVO, recognisable by their Borts applied in light blue and outlined in black, as became the norm from the mid-1950s. Although developed on the basis of the MiG-15, which was already designed for interception of bombers at high altitudes, by the mid-1950s the MiG-17 began showing its limitations – primarily during several attempts to intercept high-flying RB-47s of the USAF. (Albert Grandolini Collection)

airfields. According to the Americans, they were first intercepted by a trio of MiGs, but the Soviets departed without undertaking any action. Then, as they approached Arkhangelsk, six MiGs showed up, of which four made firing passes one after the other. The third attacker was met with return fire but the RB-47's tail guns jammed after just two seconds; yet it was enough for the MiG to hastily break off the engagement. Lastly, the fourth MiG made its attack scoring a single hit with a cannon shell passing through the left wing and exploding in the fuselage. This could have been catastrophic, for the projectile burst in the vicinity of one of the fuel tanks, but luckily its effectiveness was limited; only the intercom was knocked out and the radio damaged such that it would transmit only on one channel. Subsequently this formation of MiGs flew away, being replaced by another trio. Two MiGs tried their luck, but their fire was off the mark, while the third did not attack at all but instead flew in formation alongside the RB-47 for a few minutes. In the meantime, the Americans were over Finland and the Soviets turned back, finally leaving them alone but, according to Captain Holt, not before the third MiG's pilot gave them a salute. Available Russian sources describe the unfolding action somewhat differently.[21] Two MiG-17 fighters of the 1619th IAP, flown by Senior Lieutenants Zhiganov and Kitaychik, spotted the violator in the vicinity of Severomorsk with the foreign aircraft flying around 4,500 metres higher. Ordered by ground control, they jettisoned their external fuel tanks and climbed to engage. The MiGs caught up with the US aircraft in the vicinity of Afrikanda (considering it is located in the far north, a humorous reaction to the name is all but inevitable) and opened fire from a distance of around 800–1,000 metres with the Americans replying in kind after their first volley. Despite a lengthy chase and expending all their ammunition, the Soviets were unable to bring the US aircraft down. In addition, Captain Kurbatov of the 614th IAP was also able to intercept – almost, since he did not get closer than about 2,000 metres – but his fire from such a long distance proved ineffective. Obviously, the US and Soviet versions of events differ considerably in the details, yet it remains that the MiGs failed in their efforts while the Americans got away.

Escaping the Soviets' reach did not end the Americans' woes yet. They soon found themselves to be low on fuel. A KC-97 tanker aircraft was waiting for them off Norway but since the RB-47 failed to arrive on schedule from what the tanker's crew thought was a 'training mission', it flew away. Captain Austin heard over the radio that the tanker was leaving the orbit area while his efforts to communicate with it failed due to their transmitter being damaged. Now it seemed that having run the gauntlet of Soviet MiG attacks, the aircraft, with the photo-intelligence it gathered at great risk, would be lost due to something as simple as running out of fuel. However, the Americans had a lucky day: calling via the only frequency he was able to transmit upon, Captain Austin managed to get a tanker pilot to launch from the RAF base at Mildenhall. Tanker pilot Jim Rigley recognised Austin by his voice, which was enough for him to take off. He did so in great haste without permission or any other formalities. Subsequently, the Base Commander threatened him with court martial and British Air Traffic Control gave him a violation, but both were 'fixed' personally by General LeMay. Having met with the tanker and refuelled, the B-47 was able to reach Fairford, where it landed. Once on the ground the aircraft's battle damage prompted its crew chief to ask Captain Austin: 'What the hell kind of seagull did you hit?'

The mission described was arduous but not in vain, for the photographic material obtained was both of good quality and considerable intelligence value. All three crewmembers of the RB-47H involved were decorated with two Distinguished Flying Crosses each. When General LeMay presented the medals to the airmen, he was somewhat apologetic that decorations of a higher order were not awarded but explained that a recommendation for the Silver Star had to be approved in Washington, which could cause two problems: first they would get it 'screwed up', and secondly, 'I'd have to explain this mission to too damn many people who don't need to know.' As for Soviet defensive efforts, General LeMay inquired why the RB-47 was not shot down, to which Captain Austin replied that there was no doubt in his mind the MiG-17 pilots could have shot it down, if they had been willing to come right up the tailpipes. In response, General LeMay stated that he was 'convinced that most fighter pilots are basically cowards anyway.' In all fairness, the MiG-17 had a hard time keeping up with the RB-47 at the altitude and speed the latter flew, which obviously negatively affected their gunnery as well. Thus, the Soviet pilots' failure did not result from a lack of skill or spirit but rather from the limitations of their mounts. In addition, General LeMay also said, 'There are probably several openings today in command positions there, since you were not shot down.' He was spot on with this remark for the commander of the Soviet Northern Fleet's aviation, General Ivan Borzov, who was responsible for air defence in the area where the RB-47's mission took place, was relieved of his post.[22] He was transferred to head a training establishment but did not stay long in 'purgatory', with his career resuming with new command assignments by the end of the following year.

Arguably, this was the proverbial straw which broke the camel's back, for not long after this failure it was decided to reorganise air defences and establish the PVO as a separate branch of the Soviet Armed Forces, as described in Chapter 2.

9
NOT ALL QUIET ON THE FAR EASTERN FRONT

While overflights by foreign aircraft of the USSR's interior, and corresponding Soviet efforts to counter them were ongoing, incidents along the country's periphery also continued to occur, particularly in the Far East. Despite the Korean War being effectively ended by an armistice in 1953, the situation there remained strained. Since there was much in the Soviet Far East warranting US aerial intelligence gathering and reconnaissance, efforts continued involving aircraft from the USAF, ranging from RF-86 Sabres to RB-47 Stratojets, as well as USN aircraft. Naturally, the Soviets would physically oppose them when an opportunity to use force presented itself. As a result, the mid-1950s saw another string of Cold War incidents in the Far East leading to losses of American reconnaissance aircraft and casualties among their crews, but also to the Soviets scoring an 'own goal' so to say.

Four Shootdowns and an Unresolved Mystery

Patrol Squadron Six (VP-6), which had been previously 'blooded' in skirmishes with the Soviets, took another loss on 4 September 1954. That day P2V Neptune BuNo 128357, assigned to the squadron, took to the air from Atsugi for a reconnaissance mission over the Sea of Japan. The aircraft was tracked by Soviet radars when it came within their range, and according to American COMINT intercepts was declared 'hostile' by the Soviets as it set a course leading straight for their airspace.[1] What happened next was the subject of controversies which are not unusual in such cases. A note drawn up by the Soviet Foreign Ministry dated 8 September 1954 claimed that the US aircraft violated Soviet airspace in the vicinity of Ostrovnoy Cape, east of Nakhodka.[2] Needless to say, the Americans denied an airspace violation. Allegedly, the Americans were the first to have shot at approaching Soviet fighters whereupon the latter returned fire. Subsequently, the US aircraft flew off in the direction of the open sea. During this aerial encounter the Neptune received crippling damage, ditching into the water in the general area where the RB-29 had been lost on 13 June 1952 and the RB-50 had been lost on 29 July 1953. Unfortunately, Ensign R. H. Reid lost his life in the process (he was posthumously awarded the Navy and Marine Corps Medal) but the remaining nine crewmen made it to a life raft and were later rescued from the sea by a US Air Force SA-16 amphibian. The Neptune's demise was caused by two MiG-17s of the 22nd IAP flown by Captain N. Serebryakov and Captain P. Kasyanov.[3] According to American intercepts of Soviet communications, one of the Soviet fighters was damaged in the encounter but made it back to the airfield.[4] For their actions, the Soviet pilots were awarded the Order of the Red Banner.[5]

Chronologically, the next shootdown took place on 7 November 1954, the day when the Soviets annually celebrated the anniversary of the October Revolution (the Bolshevik coup).[6] On that day, the victim was a RB-29 (42-94000) reconnaissance aircraft of the 6007th Composite Group, which flew missions during the Korean War with the 91st Strategic Reconnaissance Squadron. This aircraft bore the name 'Tiger Lil', featuring prominent nose art in form of an attractive female clad in a tiger-striped bikini (subsequently, this was removed).[7] The Soviet narrative, as far as can be ascertained from available sources, featured the 'standard' accusations of airspace violation and opening fire by the Americans at intercepting Soviet aircraft – MiG-15s of the 610th IAP flown by Captain Kostin and Senior Lieutenant Serebryakov.[8] The attack took place in the general area where the RB-29 44-61815 was shot down on 7 October 1952. Even before being physically attacked, the Americans turned towards the Japanese island of Hokkaido. However, this did not prevent the MiG pilots from making two firing passes, of which the second resulted with one of the RB-29's wing tanks being hit. The Americans did not return fire and since their mount started to burn out of control the entire crew bailed out. All US airmen floated down under their parachutes into the sea below. Unfortunately, the navigator, 2nd Lieutenant Sigfredo Angulo got entangled in his parachute lines after hitting the water and drowned. The remaining crewmen were rescued from the sea by fishing boats or other vessels, were safely brought to the Japanese shore and subsequently picked up by US military officials sent there for that purpose. The now-unmanned RB-29 continued to fly long enough to crash inland at Nemuro, Japan, coming down onto a house which was fortunately devoid of any dwellers. The shootdown described was followed by the usual exchange of notes and protests between the Soviet Union and the United States as well as Japan. What was less usual is that the US Congress Republican leader, William Knowland, was so outraged by the incident that he demanded a break of diplomatic relations with the Soviet Union over – what he initially believed – was an unprovoked attack against an American aircraft. In response, the US President Dwight Eisenhower invited him to the White House to let him know that the aircraft's mission was not necessarily 'innocent' in nature.[9]

In practically all the previously described cases of US reconnaissance aircraft being shot down, it could be at least established with certainty, or a high probability, that they fell victim to Soviet fighters, even if there were doubts – in some cases not fully resolved to this very day – about the fate of their crews. However, what happened to RB-47 (51-2054) of the 4th Strategic Reconnaissance Squadron, lost on 18 April 1955, remained an open question until the end of the Cold War. This aircraft, crewed by Major Lacie C. Neighbors, Captain Robert N. Brooks and Captain Richard E. Watkins Jr. took off from Eielson AFB, Alaska, for a reconnaissance mission and disappeared in the blue yonder. Nothing was heard of it for decades and while the Americans suspected the aircraft was shot

Some of the crew of P2V Neptune BuNo 131515 of VP-9, brought down by PVO MiGs on 22 June 1954. Chief Radioman Jenke has his head bandaged, while Lieutenant (Junior Grade) Lockhart (second right) is seen on crutches following that encounter. (US Navy)

A P2V Neptune of VP-9, seen in 1955. Note the barbettes with 20mm guns installed in the nose and the tail, and another with two 0.50 cal machine guns atop of the fuselage: all were highly important for the self-defence of aircraft that regularly exchanged fire with PVO interceptors. (US Navy)

down by the Soviets, evidence for this remained inconclusive.[10] The aircraft's fate was only confirmed once USRJC commenced its work.[11] According to information obtained by the Commission from the Russians, it was shot down by Soviet fighter aircraft some 32 miles east of Cape Kronotski (approximately 55° north, 164° east), that is, a point well outside Soviet territorial waters and airspace. Arguably, this was the reason the Soviets did not lodge a protest about an airspace violation nor make any other statement concerning this event; it was as if it did not take place at all. An explosion, which must have been the US aircraft's final moment, was observed from a Soviet fishing trawler but no-one sighted any parachutes, there was no (not even anecdotal) evidence of any survivors and no bodies were recovered, with the Soviets picking only a few pieces of flotsam from the surface of the sea. Meanwhile, the Americans mounted a substantial search and rescue effort but were unable to find any trace of the aircraft or its crew. In view of this, the only thing left was to issue a presumptive finding of death for the three airmen which was done by the US Air Force on 17 April 1955.

According to Russian sources, the Stratojet fell prey to Captain Rubtsov and Captain Venediktov flying MiG-15bis fighters of the 865th IAP.[12] The actions of both MiG pilots were obviously highly rated by their superiors since the former was decorated with the Order of the Red Banner and promoted to major while the latter received the Order of the Red Star.

Each year the anniversary of Operation Barbarossa (the German attack against the Soviet Union) was solemnly commemorated in the USSR. The 14th anniversary of this event, 22 June 1955, saw it being 'fittingly honoured' by two MiG-15 pilots, Senior Lieutenant Teryayev and Lieutenant Filyutin of the 564th IAP, who on that day pounced upon a USN reconnaissance aircraft over the Bering Straits.[13] The American aircraft was a P2V Neptune (131515) belonging to Patrol Squadron Nine (VP-9) which took off from Naval Air Station Kodiak for what was described as a routine patrol mission over the Bering Straits.[14] While flying some 40 nautical miles west of Saint Lawrence Island, the Neptune was attacked by the MiGs which made one firing pass, and as a result its left engine caught fire. It proved impossible to put the fire out but fortunately Lieutenant Fischer, who was the aircraft's commander, managed to reach Saint Lawrence Island where he made a belly lending. While sliding on the ground, one of the Neptune's fuel tanks burst resulting in an uncontrollable blaze which consumed the aircraft. Out of the 11-man crew, seven were wounded in the MiG attack, suffered burns or were otherwise injured but luckily all manged to escape with their lives. Initially assisted by local residents, they were subsequently evacuated by an USAF transport aircraft. The story had an interesting epilogue since for the first time in the short but eventful history of such US-Soviet incidents, the Soviets expressed regret and offered partial compensation. While noting that this fell short of what might have been expected, considering the circumstances, the US side nevertheless accepted it.

In addition to the incidents already described, yet another US reconnaissance aircraft was lost on 10 September 1956. The aircraft in question was a USAF RB-50 (47-133) of the 6091st Reconnaissance Squadron which took off from Yokota AFB in Japan for its final mission. No trace of the aircraft or its crew was ever found and no distress signal from it was received either. Intelligence available at that time seemed to have indicated Soviet involvement but it was far from conclusive.[15] The next best option was to assume that the aircraft fell victim to Typhoon Emma which was raging in the general area. As things stood, not much could be done but to issue a presumptive finding of death for the crew, this being effected on 31 December 1956. Lest the men be forgotten, they are: Major Lorin C. Disbrow, Captain Rodger A. Fees, Captain William J. McLaughlin, Captain Partridge P. Taylor, First Lieutenant Peter J. Rahaniotes, Second Lieutenant Richard T. Kobayashi, TSGT Palmer D. Arrowood, SSGT Raymond D. Johnson, SSGT Paul W. Swinehart, SSGT Tehodorus J. Trias, A1C John E. Beisty, A1C William H. Ellis, A1C Wayne J. Fair, A1C Harry S. Maxwell and A1C Leo J. Sloan. Once circumstances allowed for it, the case of the missing aircraft and its crew was taken up by the USRJC. Yet despite apparent Russian cooperativeness, no new information regarding possible Soviet involvement emerged.[16] Such an outcome of investigative work is obviously far from satisfying; however, bar some new revelation it appears the fate of RB-50 (47-133) and its sixteen-man crew will remain an unresolved mystery for the foreseeable future.

Freak Fratricide

As has been repeatedly demonstrated, the Soviets put some effort into dealing with American reconnaissance aircraft and would not shy away from firing upon them if they judged that the situation warranted the use of force. However, these endeavours sometimes led to results which were as unexpected as they were unwelcome. It was already getting dark on 3 December 1954 when two MiG-15bis fighters of the 535th IAP caught up with an aircraft they were tasked to intercept. This aircraft was not replying to any queries, therefore it must have been a foreign intruder that had to be dealt with. Captain P. Byvshev, who piloted the leading MiG, wasted little time, promptly shooting it down with cannon fire.[17] Despite the approaching darkness, it was clearly visible that the downed aircraft had two engines, one under each wing. Thus, it was probably a Canberra or rather an RB-57, for the American 'clone' of the British bomber and reconnaissance aircraft was more likely to be encountered in the Far East. In any case, decisive action by Soviet fighters had put a swift end to a violation of the country's airspace – or so it seemed.

Meanwhile, an aircraft and its crew had gone missing. It so happened that on 3 December 1954, a formation of Tupolev Tu-14 bombers (ASCC/NATO-codename 'Bosun'), of the 49th MTAP was running a training sortie over the waters of the Peter the Great Gulf. Unfortunately, the last aircraft failed to return, and it soon became obvious that some calamity must have befallen it. Despite a search over the waters where the exercises were taking place, nothing of the Tupolev and its crew was found. For this reason, the men who flew it: pilot Lieutenant V. N. Muzhzhavlov, navigator Lieutenant Yu. G. Makrichuk and radio operator–gunner sailor (49th MTAP was a naval aviation unit) Ye. N. Vasilyuk were declared to be deceased.[18] Their symbolic funeral was held with empty coffins being lowered into graves while the aircraft was stricken from the unit's inventory. This should have closed the case – at least in the eyes of a casual observer.

However, the Soviet military command quickly put two and two together, realising that the shot-down 'intruder' and their own lost torpedo bomber must have been one and the same aircraft. The fact that the former reportedly had two engines, just as the latter did, was an obvious giveaway. Some technical failure must have prevented the Tupolev's crew from responding to queries which in turn led to it being taken for a foreign intruder, while poor visibility resulting from approaching darkness did the rest. Yet Soviet top brass decided not to make much out of it. For one thing, publicising such a failure would have been equal to admitting an inability to coordinate aerial activity in their own airspace. The ease with which one could get shot down would have been also very demoralising for aircrews. For similar reasons, no action was undertaken against Captain Byvshev, for he made what can be called an honest mistake, even if one of grave consequences. Had punishment been doled out, other fighter pilots might waver, thinking that the aircraft they were intercepting may be one of their own, and they had to remain combative and resolute.

The incident described was hardly among the Soviet Union's most tightly guarded secrets but for reasons outlined above it was not overtly advertised either. When the USSR was no more and it could be openly talked about, few seemed interested due to the passage of time. Yet some new details still managed to come to light. In present day Russia, professional, semi-professional and amateur battlefield archaeology as well as aviation archaeology have found considerable popularity. The *poiskovy* (literally, searchers) as they are called have been invaluable, with their findings shining new

The Tupolev Tu-14 was an unsuccessful contender to the well-known Ilyushin Il-28 – but proved better suited for naval operations, thanks to its longer range. Only 147 were ever manufactured and they served as torpedo-bombers with the Soviet Naval Aviation. (Albert Grandolini Collection)

light on historic events, uncovering the remains of numerous men who had been declared missing in action, excavating many artefacts including rare models of military hardware and so on; and they also played a role in this case. They discovered the wreckage of the Tu-14 and the remains of its crew on the slopes of Mount Lysyy Ded. Obviously, the Tupolev, despite receiving crippling hits, flew on for some time before it finally crashed. The aircraft and its crew remained missing for decades because it had been searched for over water rather than inland.[19]

10
OVERFLIGHTS CONTINUE AND THE U-2 ENTERS THE GAME

Cold War aerial reconnaissance was a dangerous game with blood being shed and tensions racked up, as clearly demonstrated by the events of the early 1950s. An effort to change this lamentable state of affairs was certainly worth a try. With that in mind, on 21 July 1955, the US President Dwight D. Eisenhower made an 'Open Skies' Proposal in Geneva, Switzerland, the essence of which was a system of disarmament and inspection effected by aerial reconnaissance of the Soviet Union by the United States and vice versa.[1] This proposal, while promising to ease Cold War tensions which in theory should have been mutually beneficial, was nevertheless rejected by the Soviet Union. While seemingly illogical and implying hostile intent on their behalf, the Soviets had their reasons: first of all, there would have been technical difficulties to implement it, in particularly for the Soviets. Theoretically this issue was addressed: President Eisenhower's proposal included the provision 'within our countries facilities for aerial photography to the other country'. However, while the Americans were able to furnish such provision, the Soviets probably would have had problems effectively using them and in addition likely could not reciprocate, at least not on the same level. Even more important, in fact crucial, was another fact which the Americans were likely to find out had the proposal been accepted. Namely, that the Soviet bomber fleet was incapable of anything but token attacks against the US mainland.[2] With the development of an intercontinental ballistic missile arsenal still many years away, this Soviet weakness could be an invitation for an American strategic nuclear attack with little fear of heavy retaliation. Considering the stance of General Curtis LeMay, who was in charge of the USAF's SAC, this was not some sort of Soviet paranoia but a realistic possibility[3] especially since plans to this end, such as the controversial 'Dropshot', had been drawn up.[4] In any case, from an American point of view, Soviet rejection of the 'Open Skies' proposal necessitated the continuation of deep penetration aerial reconnaissance missions over the USSR.

Faux Pas

As things stood, the United States continued its aerial reconnaissance of the Soviet Union which led to an incident, this time not in the air but on the ground. On 24 June 1956 a grand air show took place at the Tushyno airfield in the vicinity of Moscow. Among those invited was an American delegation headed by the US Air Force Chief of Staff, General Nathan F. Twining. Subsequently, the US delegation attended a banquet with Nikita Khrushchev, who was at that time the Soviet Union's leader.[5] What started amicably quickly degenerated into outright hostility as Khrushchev's tendency to rant and boast got the better of him (for neither the first nor the last time) leading him to point blank threaten the Americans: he boasted that Soviet fighters would shoot down US reconnaissance aircraft. Certainly, airspace violations by American aircraft were a valid cause for complaint; however, the manner and occasion of Khrushchev's remarks were certainly undiplomatic. The thus-far friendly atmosphere of the US visit was instantly spoiled and for the reminder of the Americans' stay, their Soviet hosts were trying to somehow undo the damage done by their leader's faux pas.[6] Khrushchev's outburst was caused by continuous airspace violations

As of the mid-1950s, Boeing B-47 Stratojet bombers – four of which can be seen in this photograph – were the centrepiece of the US strategic strike capability. 'Reconnaissance' operations like Homerun, run from late March into early May 1956, were undertaken by reconnaissance versions of this bomber, but they also probed blind spots and reaction times of the PVO, and thus sought for suitable approach routes. (Albert Grandolini Collection)

A pair of KC-97 Stratotankers, providing in-flight refuelling for a pair of B-47s in same fashion as they supported RB-47s during Operation Homerun. (Albert Grandolini Collection)

Operation Homerun resulted in the USAF obtaining valuable intelligence on the Yakovlev Yak-25, a then-brand-new, radar-equipped interceptor in the process of entering service with the PVO. (Albert Grandolini Collection)

and overflights of Soviet territory such as those described below. The largest and most ambitious operation of that kind thus far was conducted between 21 March and 10 May 1956. During this period of time, under the codename Homerun, 16 RB-47Es of the 10th Strategic Reconnaissance Squadron, Lockbourne AFB, Ohio, flew a series of reconnaissance flights with five RB-47Hs from the 343rd Reconnaissance Squadron, Forbes AFB, Kansas supported by 28 KC-97 tankers. Operating from Thule in Greenland, their missions covered the entire Arctic coastline of the Soviet Union which ran on an arc from the Kola Peninsula in the west to the Bering Strait in the Far East. Usually operating in tandem, two RB-47s flew through their assigned sectors with the support of two KC-97 tankers for in-flight refuelling. On 6–7 May 1956, six RB-47Es conducted a 'mass flight', entering the Soviet Union's airspace at Ambarchik and flying east to Anadyr. The overflights were of course detected but the Soviets lacked the means to effectively oppose them, since their air defences in the north were weak and spread over a large area. Frequent protests would only be an admission of impotence; nevertheless, they were occasionally made. As a standard, the US would reply that 'if' there had been 'an' overflight, it was caused by navigational error and was deeply regretted.[7] Stratojets were not the only aircraft penetrating Soviet airspace. A noteworthy mission was flown by a trio of RB-57s in the Far East. Operating from Yokota air base in Japan on 11 December 1956, they separately overflew three locations in the vicinity of Vladivostok. This overflight resulted in a particularly strong Soviet protest issued four days later on the 15 December. It read:

> On December 11, 1956, between 1307 and 1321 o'clock, Vladivostok time, three American jet planes, type B-57, coming from the Sea of Japan, south of Vladivostok, violated the airspace of the Soviet Union. Good weather prevailed in the area violated, with good visibility, which precluded any possibility of the loss of orientation by the fliers during their flight. The Government of the Soviet Union insists that the Government of the USA, take measures to punish the guilty parties and to prevent any future violations of the national boundaries of the U.S.S.R. by American planes.[8]

All the while various other small-scale projects (programs) as well as singular missions were taking place, flown not only by Americans but also by the British. Most of the time these missions did not result in airspace violations or other incidents, nor were they particularly noteworthy in this context. That said, occasionally

The crew of a PVO Yak-25 interceptor, seen in front of their mount while wearing their winter working uniforms, necessary due to harsh climatic conditions at air bases close to the polar circle. (Albert Grandolini Collection)

important data was collected, such as for example during an October 1956 (the exact date was not specified) RAF mission when valuable intelligence on the new Yak-25 interceptor was gained during a combined Washington and Canberra sortie into the Barents Sea.[9]

American overflights causing the Soviet leader's ire were a real problem while his threatful boasts remained just that: boasts. Khrushchev was understandably frustrated by the inability of Soviet air defences to deal with deep penetrations of USSR airspace. He was soon to find out that things were only going to get worse. A new player was about to enter the game, changing it even more to the Soviet's detriment.

A New Player Enters the Game

Meanwhile, efforts put into the development of a new American high-altitude reconnaissance aircraft, the Lockheed U-2, bore fruit: by mid-1956 it was ready for its first operational sortie.[10] Accordingly, the first high-altitude photographic reconnaissance mission, Mission 2003, was flown by a U-2 on 20 June 1956.[11] The aircraft piloted by Carl K. Overstreet took off from Wiesbaden in West Germany, flew over Czechoslovakia and Poland, skimmed East Germany before finally returning to Wiesbaden without incident. Two more sorties, Missions 2009 and 2010, are known to have been flown over Eastern Bloc countries on the same day, 2 July 1956. Thus, the merits of the U-2 as a high-altitude photoreconnaissance platform were proven; however, it also transpired that the aircraft were detected by radar, dashing any hopes of conducting the overflights unobserved. Successful operations over Soviet satellite states were valuable, yet it was clear that the real prize was to obtain photographic intelligence of the Soviet Union itself. Before such missions could be flown, two things had to get out of the way first: the weather over the Soviet Union had to improve and the aforementioned US Air Force delegation visiting Moscow at that time had to return. When both these conditions were met, the first U-2 mission over the Soviet Union, Mission 2013, was flown by Harvey Stockman on 4 July 1956. The American pilot flew over East Germany, across Poland and into Belorussia far past Minsk before heading north to Leningrad, overflying the Baltic Republics, the Polish coast, crossing East Germany and finally reaching West German airspace. Soviet radars detected the intruder and a massive aerial hunt ensued: in all, no fewer than 132 fighters of various types were scrambled but all efforts to intercept were in vain.[12]

The next day, 5 July 1956, Mission 2014 was flown by Carmine Vito who took the U-2 as far as Moscow and beyond, this being the only time the Soviet capital was actually overflown in the course of a deep penetration reconnaissance mission. The SAM sites ringing Moscow – while theoretically already in service – were in fact unprepared to engage at a moment's notice. After this incident they were brought to combat readiness with 'live' missiles ready on the launchpads. However, their chance to prove themselves was missed and as far as it is known, the S-25 never again had the opportunity to be fired in anger. Despite 115 of their number taking to the air, fighter aircraft proved to be powerless.[13] Moreover, efforts to intercept the elusive high-altitude intruder turned to farce when on 6 June, two Soviet MiGs were guided by ground control onto each other.[14] Two overflights, Missions 2020 and 2021, were conducted within the fame of Operation Touchdown on 9 July 1956. Again, the Soviets scrambled a large number of fighters, 125 to be precise,[15] and once more their efforts proved fruitless and almost resulted in the loss of one of their own. A MiG-19 flown by Captain Pikalin suffered an engine fire due to a fuel leak but he managed to nurse his stricken mount to an airfield.[16] Yet another overflight, Mission 2023, took place on 10 July 1956. The Soviets scrambled more than 60 fighters of various types, and a few pilots caught a glimpse of the intruder from a large distance, but their descriptions of the aircraft they barely sighted were contradictory and thus for all practical purpose useless.[17] Worse – one of the fighters, a MiG-19, ran out

'Article 341' was the first U-2: like the entire CIA-operated fleet of the time, it wore no camouflage colours and no national markings. While this jet was used as a test aircraft for its entire career, other U-2As made a number of spectacular overflights over the USSR, frequently putting large parts of the PVO on alert, and causing hundreds of scrambles by its interceptors. (Lockheed Martin)

The massive S-25 SAM system failed to react to the overflight of Moscow by a U-2 on 5 July 1956 – the only overflight of the Soviet capitol. The system's V-300 missiles thus missed their sole opportunity to be tested in actual combat. (*Official Illustrated Guide to Moscow Anti-Aircraft Defense System*)

of fuel while on landing approach. Its pilot, Captain Kapustin, attempted an emergency landing in a nearby field but crashed into an abandoned house. He sustained serious spinal injuries and the aircraft was written off. This was the first, but not last, Soviet casualty suffered when trying to intercept the U-2.[18]

The initial series of U-2 deep penetration overflights of the Soviet Union in mid-1956 provided a wealth of intelligence for the Americans. In contrast, Soviet air defences proved powerless to stop them, though at least they were able to detect and track the intruders. To their great relief, the Soviets concluded that the useful payload of such a high-flying aircraft must be very limited: in short, it could not carry a heavy load such as a nuclear bomb and thus did not present an immediate physical threat. Still, something had to be done about the overflights. Swallowing their pride, in what amounted to a de-facto admission of impotence, the Soviets delivered an official protest demanding their cessation.[19] President Eisenhower ordered a halt to the overflights and for the time being the U-2 ceased to appear over the USSR.

A Ballooning Problem

Manned aircraft were not the only means by which aerial reconnaissance was conducted, with aerostats also being extensively utilised. As early as 1947, ostensibly for the purposes of scientific research, the US Navy began Project Skyhook which made use of very large unmanned plastic (polyethylene) balloons that could lift a useful payload to altitudes of up to 30,000 metres (over 98,000 feet).[20] Similarly, starting in the late 1940s the US Air Force opted for camera-equipped balloons, which could float across the Soviet Union using strong winds at very high altitude, initially above the reach of Soviet air defences. The idea was soon put into practice resulting in a number of projects: Moby Dick, Mogul, Genetrix, as well as others.[21]

The noticeably growing number of aerostats floating through Soviet airspace prompted efforts to bring them down. The importance of combating foreign aerostats was explicitly stated in the PVO command's directives issued on 13 January 1955 and again on 20 January 1956.[22] Even before that, the first foreign balloon, presumably US, was shot down over Ukraine, near the town of Chernivtsi in the summer of 1954 (available sources do not provide the exact date) by Captain L. I. Savichev who piloted a MiG-17P. Reportedly, the target was floating in the air at an altitude of 10,000 metres and it took him just nine rounds to destroy it; however, a few days later when trying to shoot down another balloon, he failed to do so, despite firing off 150 cannon shells.[23] Reconnaissance by means of balloons was particularly intensive in 1956, especially early in the

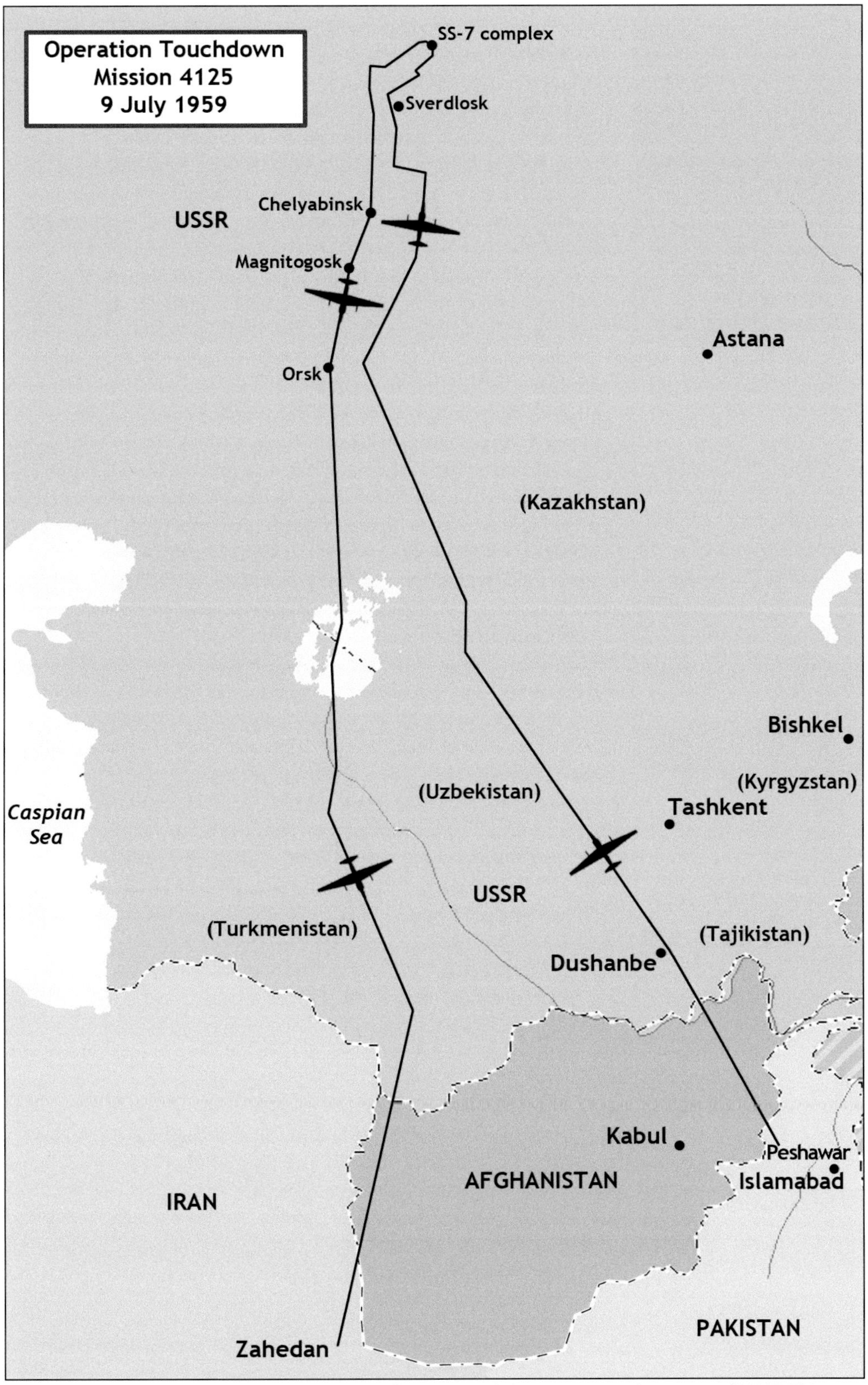

Operation Touchdown, flown by a CIA-operated U-2 on 9 July 1959 over southern central USSR. This violation of Soviet airspace prompted the PVO to scramble 125 interceptors, but these failed to catch the intruder even though it overflew several air bases and at least two S-75/SA-2 SAM sites. (Map by Tom Cooper)

year: between 1 January and 11 February, 1,476 foreign aerostats were detected in Soviet airspace[24] with the overall number reaching circa 3,000 by the year's end.[25] Certainly, it was not by coincidence that 1956 was the year Operation Genetrix was conducted,[26] even though as far as it is known, the number of balloons launched in its course was much smaller.[27] Subsequently, the number of detected and shot-down balloons declined, to grow again in 1958 and then subside with occasional spikes.[28] The combating of foreign aerostats, for a number of reasons not always an easy task, remained a feature of Soviet air defence efforts right to the very end of the USSR's existence. Among fighter pilots who had an opportunity to take a shot at them, Captain Selivanchik, who served in the 179th GIAP, was particularly successful and was credited with shooting down 13 spy balloons for which he was decorated with the Order of the Red Banner.[29] Last but not least, it is worth noting that 'balloon busting' resulted in the first entirely Soviet SAM kill taking place on 16 November 1959, when an aerostat which may have been an American WS-416L reconnaissance balloon floating at an altitude of 22,000–24,000 metres (28,000 metres was claimed; this was, however, beyond the SAM's reach) was destroyed over the Soviet Union in the vicinity of Volgograd (formerly Stalingrad) by a SA-75, but unfortunately precise details of this event are lacking.[30]

Overall, the results obtained by reconnaissance balloons were modest and hardly worth the effort. For those reasons and because they provoked the USSR's diplomatic protests, the use of spy blimps was supposedly discontinued, even though the Soviets from time to time reported shooting such down blimps. That said, there was a notable exception to the general ineffectiveness of aerostats in the reconnaissance role: namely the nuclear refining facility at Dononovo in Siberia was discovered and photographed by a Genetrix balloon.[31]

U-2 Take Two

Balloon flights, though without doubt interesting, were little more than a sideshow in the overall game played between aerial reconnaissance and air defences. Missions conducted by manned aircraft and efforts to shoot them down firmly remained the focus of both sides, especially now that the U-2 was about to re-enter the game. After an initial cessation in the summer of 1956, President Eisenhower was unwilling to approve restarting U-2 missions over the Soviet Union; however, the Hungarian crises in October and November that year, as well as his re-election by a large margin in early November 1956, led him to authorise renewed overflights of the Eastern Bloc and the USSR. The first overflight of the Soviet Union after this presidential re-authorisation was Mission 4016 flown on 20 November 1956 by a U-2 with Francis Gary Powers at the controls. Taking off from Adana in Turkey, he overflew Iran and entered Soviet airspace over

The deployment of reconnaissance balloons over the USSR, Eastern Europe and the PRC was run by the US Air Force within the frame of Project Gentrix (also known as WS-119L). It included the release of 516 high-attitude vehicles carrying AN/DMQ-1 gondolas from sites stretching all the way from Norway to Turkey. Only 54 were recovered and 31 provided useful photographs, but dozens were shot down by the PVO and allied air forces' interceptors. (US DoD)

Armenia. There, aerial photographs of Yerevan were taken before an electrical malfunction forced Powers to head back to Adana which he reached without further problems.[32] Subsequently, more U-2 missions were flown, inciting Soviet protests including the one from 15 December 1956, which, as already explained, resulted from an overflight not of U-2s but RB-57s. Yet it still resulted in the cessation of all direct American overflights including those by the U-2s, at least for the time being. However, reconnaissance flights along the Soviet periphery continued. Of the latter, especially noteworthy was Mission 4019 flown on 22 December 1956, for it was the first operational sortie by a U-2 equipped for electronic intelligence-gathering. More such missions were flown with the one conducted on 18 March 1957 resulting in a U-2 collecting electronic intelligence along the Soviet southern border, entering the country's airspace due to a compass error compounded by a slight error in the pilot's dead reckoning. Because of heavy cloud cover, the pilot, James W. Cherbonneaux, did not realise he was over the Soviet Union until he saw Soviet fighters attempting to intercept him. However, as in previous such instances, the Soviets failed once again, though one might have been close. The intruder supposedly descended down to some 10,000–11,000 metres and pilot Sidorov, in a MiG-17, got close but was ordered to abandon the chase and return to base because the target had left Soviet airspace.[33]

Finally, despite his reluctance concerning this matter, President Eisenhower was persuaded to re-authorise direct overflights of Soviet territory, which he did on 6 May 1957. Meanwhile, work was underway to make the U-2 less detectable by radar, though the measures taken failed to bring about the desired results. Of greater practical value was the fitting of improved engines which increased the U-2's maximum altitude to 74,600 feet (22,700 metres). Furthermore, new locations were added for the conduct of operations including Eielson Air Force Base in Alaska and Lahore in Pakistan. On 8 June 1957, a U-2 took off from the former location

Despite their excellent climbing capabilities, MiG-17s of the PVO never proved able to catch high-flying U-2s. (Albert Grandolini Collection)

to conduct the first intentional overflight of the Soviet Union since President Eisenhower gave his renewed approval. Missions were also flown from Pakistan, with the one conducted on 5 August 1957 yielding an important find. The U-2 piloted by Buster Edens photographed the Tyratam (Baikonur) missile and space test centre. It is interesting to note that this important discovery was made after the pilot chose to fly along a railroad track to find where it led, for it must be added that despite careful mission planning, the man in the cockpit was not left without initiative. A number of other flights took place resulting in valuable intelligence being gathered. As it retrospectively transpired, those missions flown between 4 and 27 August 1957 represented the high-water mark of U-2 overflights of the Soviet Union. Of course, noteworthy missions also took place after that time period such as when on 10 September 1957 a U-2 with William Hall at the controls photographed the Soviet missile testing facility at Kapustin Yar.[34] Naturally, all this aerial reconnaissance activity provoked a spirited yet ineffective effort by the PVO. Dozens of fighters were scrambled but all their efforts were in vain. Subsequent analysis pointed, among other things, to shortcomings in the work of radar operators and ground controllers, yet the main reason for repeated failures was that the fighter aircraft in service, such as the MiG-17, Yak-25 and even the supersonic MiG-19, simply lacked the necessary performance to intercept the high-flying intruder.[35]

According to the available sources, US President Dwight Eisenhower was against reckless moves including aerial reconnaissance operations which would be unnecessarily aggressive or provocative, regardless of what other top American military, intelligence or government officials advocated.[36] Instead, he authorised such only to the extent he perceived as essential for the security of the United States. On more than one occasion, President Eisenhower was not only willing, but actually enforced, the suspension of overflights of the Soviet Union which he judged to be needlessly provocative or possibly leading to an uncontrollable escalation. He was also very cautious of domestic as well as international public opinion and strived to avoid actions which could have resulted in a negative perception of the United States as an aggressor. In short, while at times it might have looked different from the eastern side of the Iron Curtain, if presently available records are anything to go by, reconnaissance overflights of the USSR during President Eisenhower's term in office were not intended to be 'war mongering', to use this Soviet expression.

11
CAUCASIAN CLASHES

The year 1958 was arguably another 'hot' one as far as Cold War aerial encounters were concerned. On 10 July that year, a USAF RB-50 exchanged gunfire with PVO interceptors somewhere off Petropavlovsk, though fortunately no damage or casualties were reported. Several months later, on 31 October, a Soviet fighter attempted to intercept a USAF RB-47 on patrol over the Black Sea. A few days had barely passed when, on 4 November, an interceptor of the PVO harassed an American C-130 transport over the Sea of Japan.

November was even more eventful. On the 7th of that month: in the vicinity of Gotland in the Baltic, a USAF RB-47 was fired on by a Soviet fighter, while literally at the other end of the world another RB-47 was 'buzzed' by a PVO interceptor over the Sea of Japan.[1] According to Russian sources, the first alleged violation of Soviet airspace that year had already taken place on 2 March 1958.[2] The Soviets apparently showed little concern for most of the incidents mentioned except the ones which resulted in shots being fired. Regarding the July incident, the Soviets claimed that an American aircraft violated the USSR's maritime border circa 150 kilometres south of Petropavlovsk-Kamchatsky. The US aircraft flew away after warning shots were fired by an intercepting Yak-25 fighter of the 865th IAP.[3] Similarly, on 7 November a Soviet MiG-17 fighter flown by Major Nadpyuchiyevy intercepted a US RB-47 which was, if not outright over Soviet territorial waters in the Baltic, then very close to them. According to the Soviets, the Americans opened fire first, to which the Soviet pilot replied in kind but it did not pursue the US aircraft as it flew away.[4] The latter incident brought about an exchange of notes between the USA and the USSR, with the US claiming that at the time of the incident the American aircraft was approximately 66 miles away from the nearest Soviet territory.[5] As can be seen, Cold War aerial encounters were taking place around the USSR's entire periphery but nowhere did they result in shootdowns except in the Caucasus where, within a timespan of little over two months, US aircraft were brought down twice.

The year 1958 saw numerous encounters between interceptors of the POV and US reconnaissance aircraft. This MiG-17 was photographed while slowing down to maintain formation with an unknown jet intercepted close to the Soviet airspace. (Albert Grandolini collection)

An RB-47H as seen from another jet of the same variant. Notable is the giant pod slung from the starboard fuselage, and several other antennas of the AN/ALD-4 ELINT suite, which included pulse analysers and recorders. (Albert Grandolini Collection)

Exposure of CIA Secrets Barely Avoided: The Shootdown of C-118 no. 51-3822

It was already getting late on 27 June 1958 when a pair of MiG-17 fighters of the 976th IAP was scrambled from Kurdemir in Soviet Azerbaijan.[6] Guided by GCI, the MiGs flown by Captain G.F. Svetlichnikov and Senior Lieutenant B.F. Zakharov intercepted an aircraft over Soviet Armenia south of Yerevan. The aircraft was Douglas C-118 Liftmaster transport serial number 51-3822 (essentially, the military variant of the well-known DC-6) with nine men aboard: Colonel Dale D. Brannon, Major Luther W. Lyles, Major Robert E. Crans, Major Bennie A. Shupe, Captain James T. Kane, First Lieutenant James N. Luther, SSG James G. Holman, A2C Earl H. Reamer and A2C Peter N. Sabo. It was flying from Wiesbaden in West Germany, via Nicosia in Cyprus to Tehran and Karachi, in Iran and Pakistan respectively. Of note is that this particular C-118 was not an ordinary transport aircraft on a regular supply flight but was later reported to be the personal aircraft of Allen Dulles, then director of the Central Intelligence Agency, on a mission to deliver important and highly sensitive documents to the CIA base in Pakistan from where U-2 high-altitude reconnaissance aircraft operated. This was revealed over three decades later to the press by Colonel Fletcher Prouty who served as Chief of Special Operations for the Joint Chiefs of Staff under President John F. Kennedy.[7] Declassified documents show that among other items aboard the aircraft, there were two briefcases with address books containing the names, telephone numbers and addresses of CIA personnel and stations.[8] Obviously, one cannot avoid asking how could an aircraft with such a sensitive load find itself in Soviet airspace? It appears that the C-118 in question strayed over Soviet territory due to a number of factors: strong signals from Soviet radio navigation beacons, poor weather with limited visibility and finally, by confusing Lake Sevan in Armenia with Lake Van in Turkey. While the idea that the aircraft was somehow lured over Soviet territory, for example by the Soviet radio navigation signals, makes for an attractive theory, it was dismissed by US intelligence since the Soviets apparently had no idea what a prize catch almost fell into their hands.[9] Similarly, there is nothing in available Soviet sources that would confirm they had any foreknowledge about the documents the C-118 carried and hence did not plan to entrap it in an aerial ambush.

The American C-118 was intercepted by the MiGs and their pilots identified it as a transport. They requested instructions via radio on further course of action, since according to them, the US aircraft ignored their signals to follow. By pure coincidence, the commander of the Baku Air Defence District, General V. D. Ivanov, was at that district's command post and being unsure himself, he in turn contacted the main PVO command post in Moscow. The latter replied swiftly and laconically: he was to act according to circumstances. Being advised to do as he saw fit, General Ivanov ordered the US aircraft to be shot down. An unarmed piston-engine transport was no match for cannon-armed jet fighters: being repeatedly hit, the C-118 caught fire. Five men took to their parachutes: Colonel Brannon, Major Crans, Major Shupe, A2C Reamer and A2C Sabo successfully bailed out over Armenia while four crewmembers remained aboard. The C-118 was afire but still controllable and Major Lyles crash landed it on a dirt airstrip in the vicinity of Hindarkh/Hindarx in Azerbaijan. While the aircraft was consumed by flames on the ground, the four men walked away from it almost unscarred. All nine Americans were taken into custody by the Soviets, two who suffered light burns were administered the necessary medical aid, and were brought to Baku in Azerbaijan. Fast-forwarding a little, once released they gave some details to the press of how they were shot down and apprehended.[10] To begin with, Major Lyles supposedly lowered his landing gear to indicate he was to comply with the intercepting Soviet pilots' instructions, but they opened fire anyway. One re-attacked the damaged US aircraft as it was already at low altitude and about to land but fortunately missed. How much of this was Cold War propaganda, the author will leave for the readers to judge. Meanwhile, the men who bailed out were roughed-up by an Armenian mob when they reached the ground and Major Shupe was almost hanged from a telephone pole (the abuse was confirmed by classified but since released documents).[11] Perhaps they were mistaken by the locals for Turks. In any case, the very dangerous situation was defused in a rather surprising way: by loudly shouting names of such locations in the US as New York and Chicago, Major Shupe convinced his tormentors that he and the others were Americans. From that point on, the crowd became visibly less hostile, but the Americans were safe only when Soviet security forces arrived at the scene, taking them into custody.

The nine Americans held in Baku were of course interrogated but not in a forceful way. The Soviets failed to obtain any compromising information from them, while all sensitive materials which were aboard the ill-fated C-118 were destroyed when the aircraft burned up on the ground. What was not consumed by flames was disposed of by other means: Major Shupe ripped up all classified documents he had on him and then devoured them one by one while still under the parachute.[12] The Soviets were a little suspicious but without the physical evidence which was destroyed with the aircraft, they had no clues as to its actual role. They only found out what a prize catch had narrowly eluded them after the end of the Cold War. Since nothing could be gained by holding them, the Soviets decided to release the Americans, which they did on 7 July 1958 at the Soviet-Iranian border. Meanwhile, an exchange of diplomatic notes between the USSR and the US took place, with the latter assuming a sterner tone once the nine Americans were out of the Soviet Union. The whole incident had one more result: namely, the Soviet Defence Ministry issued, on 4 July 1958, order no. 0049 which stated that foreign intruders were to be shot down if necessary. While foreign aircraft which were violating Soviet airspace, or merely accused of doing so by the Soviets, were being downed by Soviet fighter aircraft, until this time this had been done on an ad hoc, case-by-case manner; but from when order no. 0049 was issued, this practice was made official.

A 'Kill' On The Wedding Day – The Loss Of C-130 No. 60528

On 2 September 1958, USAF C-130A-II Hercules serial number 60-528, assigned to the 7406th Support Squadron, took off from Incirlik Air Base in Turkey on a reconnaissance mission along the Turkish-Soviet border. Aboard the aircraft were six flight crew members from the 7406th Support Squadron and 11 USAF 'back-enders' from Detachment One of the 6911th Radio Group Mobile. The US Hercules was to fly a course parallel to the Soviet border, but the aircraft was not to approach it closer than 100 miles. The aircraft's crew reported passing over Trabzon in Turkey at an altitude of 25,500 feet and acknowledged receiving a weather report, this being the last words heard from them.

Meanwhile across the border, two MiG-17 fighters of the 117th IAP, with their pilots Senior Lieutenant Kucheryaev and Senior Lieutenant Ivanov, were standing by ready to take off at a short notice from Leninakan (Giumri/Gyumri).[13] Of the two men, the first was to get married that day; however, he was ordered to report to the airfield for duty. Since an order in any military organisation is not something to be negotiated, he had to hastily postpone his personal plans. The pilots had lunch at 1400 hours and were about to take an afternoon nap when at 1430 hours the order to take to the air was issued. Both pilots swiftly manned their aircraft and took off. Once airborne, they were issued instructions on altitude, speed and all else necessary to intercept an intruder which was apparently already inside Soviet airspace and flying deeper and deeper into it by the minute. Many thoughts raced through Senior Lieutenant

A MiG 17 standing on alert, with pilot inside the cockpit, ready for take-off at short notice. (Albert Grandolini Collection)

The ill-fated C-130A Hercules serial number 60-528, shot down over Soviet Armenia on 2 September 1958. (Albert Grandolini Collection)

Senior Lieutenant Kucheryaev and Senior Lieutenant Ivanov of the 117th IAP. (*Sovetskaya Aviatsiya*)

Senior Lieutenant Gavrilov and Senior Lieutenant Loptakov of the 168th IAP. (*Sovetskaya Aviatsiya*)

A still from the gun camera film taken by Kucheryaev's MiG-17 showing his attack on the C-130 on 2 September 1958. (USRJC)

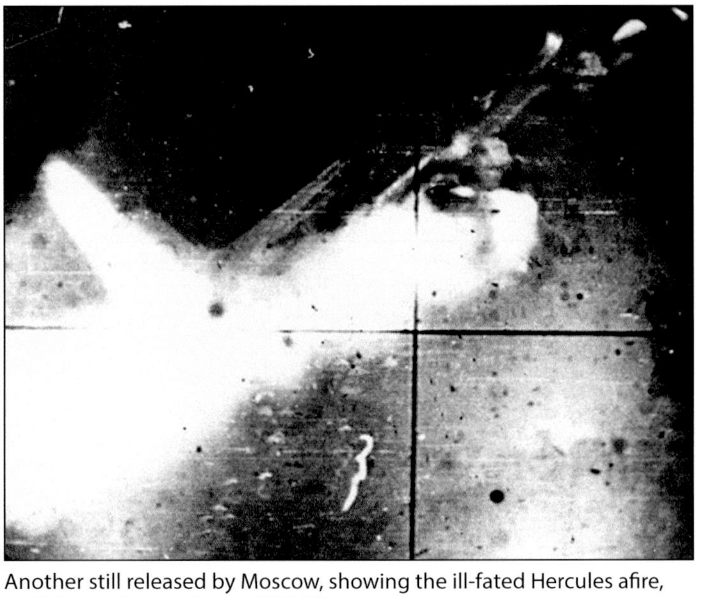

Another still released by Moscow, showing the ill-fated Hercules afire, and short of going down. (USRJC)

Kucheryaev's mind as he led the pair of MiGs towards the assigned target. He was both excited as it was obviously an actual combat mission, the interception of a real intruder, and anxious since this could be the start of an all-out war. Soon enough, he sighted the target, a large four-engine aircraft, but one he did not recognise from any of the photos of NATO aircraft he had been shown in training. However, he could clearly see its US markings which dispelled any doubts as to what he was dealing with. Senior Lieutenant Kucheryaev fired a long burst across the American aircraft's nose. As a result, the US aircraft changed its course but in such a way as to assume a heading directly towards Yerevan, the Soviet Armenia's capital. This manoeuvre sealed its fate: now ground control ordered the MiG pilots to destroy the target. Senior Lieutenant Kucheryaev manoeuvred to attain the best firing position, aimed carefully and opened fire with his MiG's cannons. It seemed to him that the US aircraft returned fire, though as it later transpired it had been unarmed. Subsequently, when analysing the gun camera footage, he realised that small parts had broken off from the targeted aircraft as a result of hits sustained and they were swirling in its slipstream, creating the impression of rounds fired from defensive armament. The MiG's cannon shells were devastatingly effective: flames and smoke started to pour from the American aircraft's right wing and starboard pair of engines. Suddenly, two other MiGs with blazing guns cut across the air in front of Senior Lieutenant Kucheryaev, forcing him to cease fire. Because the foreign aircraft was heading directly towards Yerevan, the air defence command decided to scramble another pair of MiGs from the 168th IAP based there. Their pilots, Senior Lieutenant Lopatkov and Senior Lieutenant Gavrilov, raced towards the foreign aircraft ignoring everything else, including 117th IAP's MiGs already engaging it. However, being overzealous they overshot the target with their fire being wide off the mark. Meanwhile, Senior Lieutenant Kucheryaev was able to re-engage the US aircraft, scoring additional hits which proved decisive. The target pulled up as if in a last gesture of defiance – though this must have been the result of its controls being damaged – and then plunged earthwards. Having shot the intruder down, the MiGs were first advised to orbit in the air awaiting further instructions but soon the order came to return to base. Even in times of heightened US-Soviet tensions, the shooting down of an American aircraft was an extraordinary event. Hence a special commission arrived from Moscow to investigate the matter, though much of the dirty work on the ground, such as sifting through the wreckage, was done by 117th

The rear part of the wreckage of C-130A 60-528. (USRJC)

Central part of the wreckage, including the so-called 'wing-box'. (USRJC)

IAP's personnel. The American aircraft went down near the village of Sasnashen in Soviet Armenia, circa 55 kilometres northwest of Yerevan and 20 kilometres southeast of Leninakan. It was quickly established that the shot-down US aircraft was a C-130 Hercules. The Soviets recovered a number of items from the wreckage but more importantly also claimed to have found 13 bodies at the crash site, all of which were handed over to the Americans, though this does not correspond with known facts (see below). As for the two MiG pilots who brought it down, they received a congratulatory message from the USSR's defence minister, Marshal Rodion Malinovski, which was read out in front of 117th IAP's personnel mustered for the occasion and both were presented with material rewards in the form of cameras.[14] Last but not least, Senior Lieutenant Kucheryaev finally managed get his personal matters in order as he tied the knot.

Rather surprisingly considering how secretively military operations were handled in the Soviet Union, the whole matter was described in the Soviet press. The journal *Sovetskaya Aviatsiya* (*Soviet Aviation*) published a two-part article relating an exercise involving two pairs of Soviet fighters which intercepted an aerial target.[15] First radar operators and plotters tracked this aerial target, leading a controller to order the scramble of a pair of fighters from Leninakan. It was delayed by a dust storm which may be a case of poetic licence but meanwhile another pair of fighters was scrambled from Erevan. The former flown by Senior Lieutenants Kucheryaev and Ivnaov, the latter by Senior Lieutenants Lopatkov and Gavrilov. According to the article, Senior Lieutenant Lopatkov made the first attack on the target during which he turned on his gun camera and he was followed by Senior Lieutenant Gavrilov. The target was then attacked by the other pair of fighters, after which the first pair made yet another attack against it. Subsequently, all fighter pilots returned to their bases and were congratulated by the commanding officer for successfully completing their mission, the results of which were confirmed by gun camera footage. It is noteworthy, taking into account the aforementioned Soviet secrecy, that the real names of the pilots, navigators and plotters were published, and even their photographs, and the actual locations from which they operated, were given. Even though the whole thing was described as an exercise and no mention was made that the target was a US aircraft, nor of the fact that it was destroyed, there is no doubt that what was related was in fact the shootdown of the American C-130.

Meanwhile, the Americans realised that one of their electronic reconnaissance aircraft had gone missing, prompting efforts to find out what had happened to it and its crew. The investigation conducted by the US Air Force in Europe elicited information that an aircraft identified as a C-130 was intercepted at about 1400 hours on 2 September 1958 by fighter aircraft in the vicinity of the Turkish-Soviet border. The course of the C-130 was then diverted eastward under control of the Soviet aircraft. Following this, the sound of an explosion was heard, and a column of smoke was seen rising from behind a range of hills within Soviet territory.[16] Furthermore, according to US intelligence, a flight of Soviet fighters was already in the air and it was noted that the US aircraft 'mysteriously' changed course and flew into Soviet airspace[17] – to put it in other words, that was in effect an accusation that the C-130 was purposefully and maliciously lured into Soviet airspace to be shot down by Soviet

За нашу Советскую Родину!

СОВЕТСКАЯ АВИАЦИЯ

ГАЗЕТА ВОЕННО-ВОЗДУШНЫХ СИЛ
ОРГАН МИНИСТЕРСТВА ОБОРОНЫ СОЮЗА ССР

ПЕРЕДОВЫЕ ЛЮДИ НАШЕЙ АВИАЦИИ

ВЫСОКОЕ МАСТЕРСТВО

2. Стремительная атака

Title page of the magazine *Sovetskaya Aviatsiya*, No. 222 (3084), published on 20 September 1958, including a photograph of four plotters at work (from left to right): Captain N. Romanyuta and Privates D. Pankeev, N. Budarin, and S. Ichin. (Soviet Ministry of Defence)

fighters waiting in ambush. However, there is little evidence to support this, and the most likely explanation is that similar to the C-118 incident described above, the Americans made a navigational mistake because Soviet radionavigation beacons operated on frequencies similar to those on the Turkish side of the border while emitting stronger signals. In any case, when confronted about the incident on 6 September, the Soviets denied any knowledge of it. Finally, on September 12 they claimed to have found a destroyed aircraft and the remains of six crewmen. In response to US demands for information about 11 missing crew members, the Soviets stated on 19 September that no other information on crew members was at their disposal. On 24 September, the Soviets returned six sets of remains, but, when queried, still maintained that they had no information regarding the 11 missing crewmen.[18] The Americans were obviously not satisfied with such replies, especially since US intelligence claimed to have the actual recording of the pilot's radio transmissions during the shootdown. This transmission was at times garbled and unintelligible, but the essential phrases were as follows: 'I see the target, a large one...I am attacking the target... The target is a transport, four engine...The target is burning...There's a hit!...The target is banking...I am opening fire…The tail assembly is falling off…Look at him, he will not get away, he is already falling...He is falling...The target has lost control, it is going down...The target has turned over... The target is falling...'[19] Having this at his disposal, on 13 November 1958 Deputy Under Secretary of State Robert Murphy made a lengthy verbal presentation to the Soviet ambassador Mikhail A. Menshikov. Under Secretary Murphy offered to play the recording of the radio conversation between the Soviet pilots who had shot down the C-130 for the ambassador. However, the ambassador refused to listen to it, though the US official still managed to hand him the transcript of the said recording.[20] Further attempts to gain information were made in early 1959 during Soviet Deputy Premier (Prime Minister) Anastas Mikoyan's fence-mending visit to Washington. Yet he also refused to divulge anything on the matter, stating point blank that he had no knowledge of it, somehow spoiling the otherwise positive atmosphere of the visit, as reflected by subsequent comments in the American press.[21]

As things stood during the remaining years of the Cold War, the Americans could not make any further progress regarding the loss of C-130 Hercules number 60528 and its 11 missing crewmen. It took changes of historic proportions for things to move forward. Once the Soviet Union was no more, among the issues taken up by the USRJC the case of the Hercules shot down on 2 September 1958 was high on the agenda and the Americans were able to access documents relating to the downing and its aftermath. These included, amongst other things, gun camera pictures showing the actual shootdown, photographs of the aircraft's wreckage after it went down, and a list of items found by the Soviets at the crash site: a set of orders for the flight crew, a 0.45 calibre pistol no. 1769459, some ID cards and ID tags as well as money and so on.[22] Importantly, the exact location where the Hercules went down was learned, allowing the organisation of work at the site. US research and excavation teams started their efforts in Armenia in 1993. Apart from numerous wreckage parts still littering the area, an ID tag was found that belonged to A2C Archie Bourg, a USAF airborne maintenance technician aboard 60528 when the aircraft went down. It was an encouraging find and in fact within the next few years circa two thousand human skeletal fragments were recovered in the vicinity – as it transpired, the 11 missing crewmen's bodies had been there all the time. Now all 17 men were accounted for: A2C Archie T. Bourg, Jr., Captain Paul E. Duncan, A2C James E. Ferguson, Jr., A2C Joel H. Fields, Captain Edward J. Jeruss, A2C Harold T. Kamps, A2C Gerald C. Maggiacomo, A2C Clement O. Mankins, A2C Gerald H. Medeiros, TSGT Arthur L. Mello, A2C Robert H. Moore, A2C, A1C Robert J. Oshinskie, MSGT George P. Petrochilos, SSGT Laroy Price, Captain John E. Simpson, SR Captain Rudy J. Swiestra, First Lieutenant Ricardo M. Villarreal. Their mortal remains were repatriated and the entire crew of tail number 60528 were laid to rest at Arlington National Cemetery.[23] In addition, the men were also commemorated by monuments both in Armenia and the United States.[24]

Numerous aerial incidents, including two shootdowns of American aircraft with one resulting in the loss of lives, could have made the year 1958, its summer in particular, a contender for the title 'high point of the Cold War in the air'. However, unbeknown to all parties involved, the climax was yet to come. That said, before it happened there would still be more than a year of high-altitude cat and mouse games.

12
RETURN OF THE U-2

Aerial reconnaissance of the Soviet Union continued, taking the form of peripheral flights which seldom – if at all – crossed into Soviet airspace, as well as deep penetration overflights of the USSR's territory. The U-2s were utilised in both types of operations, though exclusively in the latter. Having reached its highpoint in the summer of 1957, U-2 overflights of the Soviet Union subsequently decreased in number. Starting in 1958, they became singular events, few and far between. Despite or maybe because of that, whenever an overflight took place, it had the effect of stirring a proverbial hornets' nest, resulting in feverish Soviet interception attempts.

Kelly Johnson, designer of the U-2, and one of the resulting aircraft: a proud father and his child. The pride was for a reason, because Johnson's creation for a long time both figuratively and literally stayed above anything the PVO could put up. (Albert Grandolini Collection)

Déjà Vu

Just a single mission was conducted in 1958, when on 1 March (2 March according to Soviet/Russian sources) that year, a U-2 overflew the Soviet Far East. Soviet air defences reacted by scrambling 51 fighter aircraft of all available types: MiG-15s, MiG-17s and MiG-19s as well as Yak-25s. Predictably they failed, never coming closer than several thousand metres to the target. A few sightings were made but again because of the distance the pilots were not able to see much, with their reports as to what they saw being vague as well as contradictory and thus of no practical value. Two MiG-17 pilots even fired short bursts from their guns (in all, 14 rounds of 23mm and 37mm calibre), yet due to the distance to the target they had no chance of hitting anything. The U-2 eluded Soviet fighters once again and the latter could do nothing but return to their airfields. Even that could be problematic, for one MiG-19 burst a tyre on touch-down but did not result in a crash.[1] Subsequently, the overflight also resulted in angry exchanges and blame games between the highest echelons of the Soviet military establishment and the defence industry. All this was as frustrating as it was unproductive: only new fighter-interceptors and ground-based anti-aircraft weapon systems, the S-75 SAM in particular, could change the situation. Their entry into service was just around the corner but until that happened there was little the Soviets could do.

Obviously, the Soviets had reasons for discontent but not everyone in the US was happy with the mission either – among the latter was the President of the United States himself. The particular U-2 which flew the mission employed measures which were supposed to hide it from radar detection, but a Soviet protest delivered a few days after the overflight demonstrated that the aircraft had been detected and tracked. In view of the situation, on 7 March 1958 President Eisenhower ordered an immediate cessation of missions over the Soviet Union. This was to remain in effect until the summer of 1959.[2] President Eisenhower had numerous reasons to curtail aerial reconnaissance activity. He not only desired to ease tensions and wanted to avoid being perceived as aggressive or provocative on the domestic and world stage, but he also intended to push through a number of arms limitation and confidence-building proposals. If such things were to be effective, Soviet cooperation was needed, but it was obviously impossible to secure such cooperation as long as USSR airspace was being violated. On the one hand, the United States had reasons to keep a watchful eye on the Soviet threat, but on the other, when protesting such airspace violations as high-altitude reconnaissance overflights, the Soviets were in the right and could legitimately suspect such missions to be preparations for an attack. Furthermore, President Eisenhower was being repeatedly assured that such overflights as those made by the U-2s were as good as undetectable, yet it consistently proved not to be so. If that was not bad enough, President Eisenhower was also deceived by his own military and intelligence communities about the use of spy blimps. He found himself not only confronted by diplomatic protests but embarrassingly for the United States, the Soviets displayed American balloons which had gone down over the USSR. The US President had enough reasons to decide to halt US aerial reconnaissance activity over Soviet territory.

Yet despite all the reservations and arguments to the contrary outlined above, President Eisenhower reauthorised U-2 overflights of the USSR. To provide context, it needs to be pointed out that the Soviets had made a number of tangible achievements in the fields of rocketry and missile technology, while boasting of even more. As a result, concerns arose in the United States that the Soviet missile arsenal would eclipse the American one, both numerically and in quality; this being the so-called missile gap. This had to verified or disproven and unsurprisingly, voices arguing for a renewal of overflights of the Soviet Union mounted. Finally, the US President was convinced and approved a single such mission which took place on 9 July 1959. Subsequently, one more U-2 mission was flown on 6 December that year, noteworthy for the fact that the aircraft had a British pilot, Squadron Leader Robert Robinson, behind the controls. It was the first overflight of Soviet Territory by a U-2 with a British pilot in the cockpit, though British pilots had already flown the aircraft on missions elsewhere. Both missions were focused on the Soviet missile programme: in the case of the former, Tyratam (Baikonur), while during the second, Kapustin Yar was overflown. The Soviets again and again proved unable to effectively oppose the overflights. One can hardly escape the feeling of déjà vu: a U-2 mission reluctantly approved by the US President and futile Soviet interception attempts seemed to be a scenario locked in a perpetual cycle of repetition.

Accidental Exposure

Before moving on, one more issue deserves to be addressed. What, if anything at all, did the Soviets know about the U-2? According to the Soviet military intelligence officer Pyotr Semyonovich Popov, who offered his services to the Americans, the Soviets were in possession of the U-2's 'full technical details' – at least this is what he stated to his handlers in 1958.[3] However, if events up to 1 May 1960 are anything to go by, this claim seems to lack substance. It appears the Soviets did not even know what type of aircraft they were dealing with, for the mysterious airspace violator remained an 'intruder' or 'target' – just a blip on the radar screen which hardly anybody saw. The few sightings made were vague and contradictory; for example, one Soviet pilot reported seeing a 'Canberra'.[4] Considering how different the Canberra and the U-2 were, it is clear that he did not see much and that this, and other sightings, were practically useless. Possibly the first time the Soviets gained meaningfully visual contact with the U-2 was by a pilot from one of the units assigned to the Turkestan Military District. In February 1959, a MiG-19 was scrambled to intercept a high-flying intruder which entered Soviet airspace from the south. Using the afterburner, the MiG managed to reach an altitude of 17,500 metres. The foreign aircraft was still about 3,000 metres higher and thus out of reach but close enough for the Soviet pilot to see it. Upon returning back to base, the pilot gave a detailed account of the event and also made a sketch showing an aircraft with a slim fuselage and long wings – considering the circumstances, the U-2 was depicted fairly accurately. The report was sent up all the way to Moscow and generated enough interest for a special commission to come down from the Soviet capital and investigate the events at the scene. Yet the commission failed to take the matter seriously, concluding that the pilot involved made the story up in order to draw attention to himself and receive a reward.[5] While that story sounds plausible, it has one major weakness: as far as it is known, no U-2 overflight took place in February 1959, with only two flights over the Soviet Union being conducted on 9 July and 6 December that year, as described above. The U-2 was indeed exposed that year: not as a result of an elaborate intelligence operation but by pure accident. It so happened that on 24 September 1959, a U-2 with Thomas L. Crull at the controls was heading back to Atsugi, Japan

Initially after their service entry, neither Su-9 missile-armed interceptors nor S-75 (SA-2) SAM systems of the PVO proved capable of dealing with the U-2 – sometimes because they were not ready for action, other times because of their improper handling, and sometimes because U-2s were simply elusive. (Albert Grandolini Collection)

after a local flight. The aircraft ran low on fuel, resulting in a flameout which in turn forced the pilot to make an emergency landing at the Fujisawa glider airstrip.[6] Both the aircraft and the pilot were quickly secured and then moved away by the Americans, but the story made it to the press and appeared in Japanese newspapers the next day. Articles published described an aircraft which, if to go by its layout, was best suited for high altitude flying and also noted a window for cameras, thus hinting that it probably had a reconnaissance role. In this manner, the U-2 was revealed to the general public and thus by extension to the Soviets as well, regardless of any prior intelligence information or lack thereof. However, in practical terms this did not bring them any closer to stopping its overflights.

Close But Not Quite

The U-2 reappeared over the Soviet Union on 5 February 1960, flown by a British pilot, Squadron Leader John MacArthur. In the course of the mission, Tyratam (Baikonur) as well as Kazan were overflown and, in addition, long stretches of the Soviet rail network were photographed. At Kazan, the Tu-98 (ASCC/NATO-codename 'Backfin') bomber prototype was spotted.[7] Available Soviet sources seem to indicate that the overflight was neither seriously challenged by air defences nor did it unnerve the senior military and political leadership. One cannot help but wonder why some U-2 overflights were hardly noted while others resulted in a flurry of Soviet military and political activity. If the 5 February mission belongs to the former category of passing without note, the next overflight would be firmly in the latter.

A little over two months later, on 9 April 1960, a U-2 flown by Bob Ericson entered Soviet airspace from the south and then flew on, penetrating it deeply. Its flight path took the American aircraft over the Semipalatinsk nuclear test site, the Sary-Shag missile range, and the Tyratam (Baikonur) rocket test site, just to mention the most important installations.[8] This time, the PVO apparatus sprang into action with 31 MiG-17 and MiG-19 as well as Su-9 fighters scrambled.[9] In his memoires, Khrushchev states that SAMs were meant to shoot the intruding aircraft down but were caught unprepared and failed to engage it.[10] Fighter aviation made a serious attempt to intercept the U-2; however, among the aircraft which took to the air, only the Su-9 had a realistic chance to achieve that goal. One of the Sukhois, with Captain Doroshenko at the controls, managed to climb high enough to report visual contact with the target. Fortunately for the Americans, the Soviet pilot was unable to maintain altitude and dropped off before he could initiate a missile firing engagement sequence. The U-2 not only managed

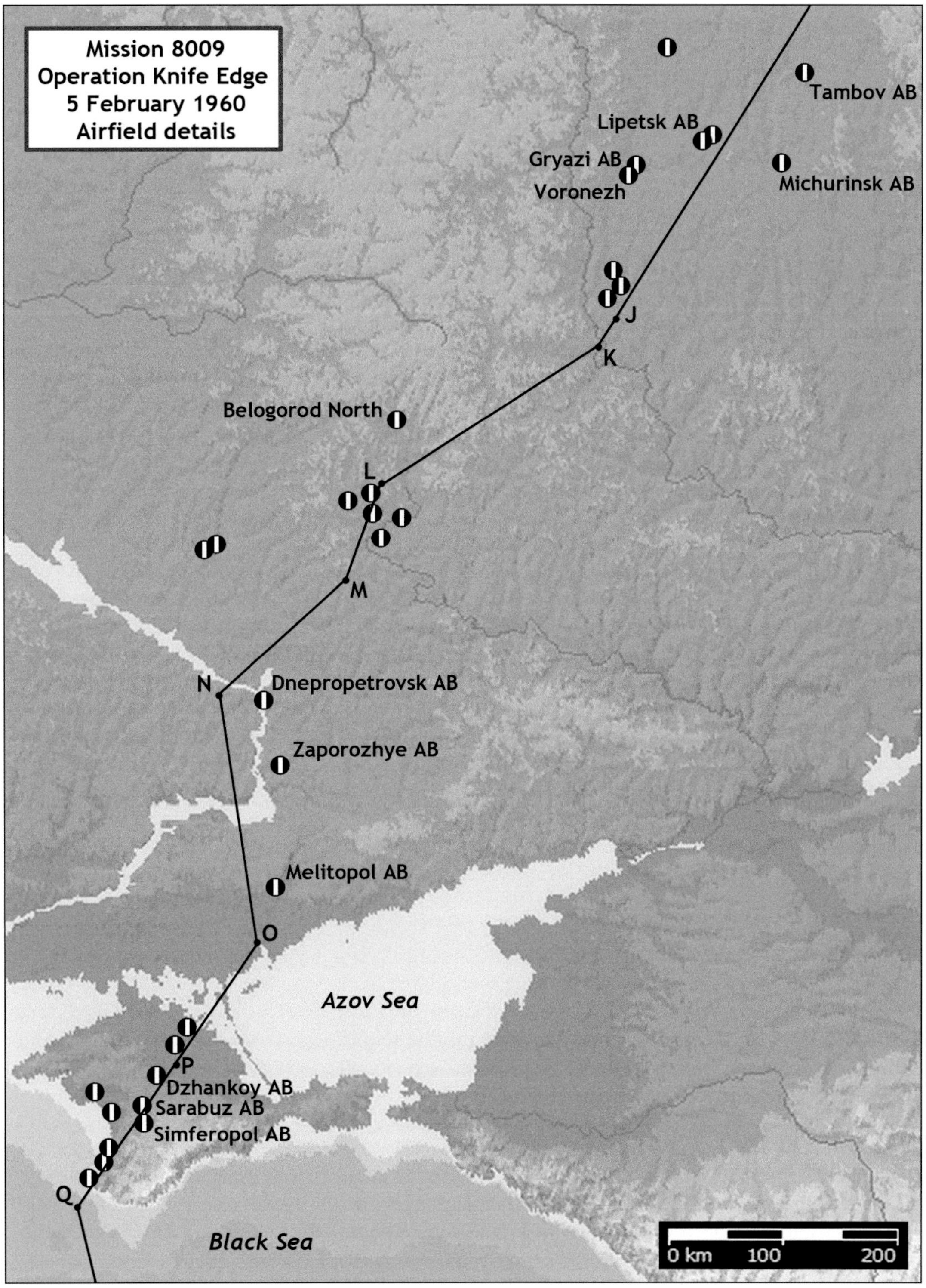

A map showing part of the route taken by Squadron Leader John MacArthur while flying a CIA-operated U-2 on 5 February 1960. MacArthur not only overflew the Tyratam (Baikonour) space launch site and Kazan on the way into the USSR, but on the way out overflew or passed close to about 30 air bases and other airfields in Ukraine alone. Nevertheless, the PVO proved unable to catch the high-flying intruder. (Map by Tom Cooper)

to escape again but to make matters worse, the Soviets also lost a MiG-19. Its pilot, Senior Lieutenant Vladimir Karchevski, ejected just before his aircraft crashed; however, that was too low for his parachute to open and he was killed as a result. The cause of the crash was never sufficiently determined, with various reasons being given ranging from fuel starvation to pilot error. Thus, the hunt for the U-2 claimed a second casualty; this time, a mortal one.[11]

Yet another unsuccessful attempt to stop the American high-altitude overflights resulted in a critical analysis of PVO actions. The mistakes of radar operators and ground controllers were noted as well as a number of other shortcomings, the most important of which was that Su-9 pilots such as Captain Doroshenko failed to make the best use of their fighters. In their defence, it should be pointed out that the interceptor was only recently accepted into service. As a result, neither ground controllers nor pilots had enough experience with the type to fully utilise its capabilities. The point is illustrated best by the fact that most pilots did not even have the opportunity to fire a live AAM in training. In the end, no-one's head rolled in the literal sense, but a number of officers were penalised. When Khrushchev learned that the U-2 had eluded air defences once again, he was furious and made it clear that another failure would not be tolerated. This time around the Soviets were close to bringing the U-2 down, even though they had not quite succeeded yet. Indeed, everything needed, such as SAMs, high-performance interceptors and so on, was available which, in turn, meant that sooner or later they were going to make fewer mistakes and finally get their prize.

13
THE END OF AN ERA

In April 1960, the Su-9 fighter-interceptor had its chance to better the U-2; come May, it would be the S-75's turn. By the end of the 1950s, the S-75 surface-to-air missile systems had already started to be deployed but were initially available in limited numbers, defending only the most important locations in the USSR; such as for example, Leningrad, Volgograd or Sverdlovsk. The deployment of SAMs at the latter location was ascertained by the CIA during US Vice-President Richard Nixon's visit to the USSR in 1959.[1] While it appears the Americans were oblivious to the fact that on 9 April the U-2 had escaped only because the Soviet pilot flying a Su-9 interceptor lacked experience in handling his aircraft, they still were not completely dismissive of potential hazards. For this reason, U-2 missions were, as a general rule, planned in such a way as to avoid known SAM sites. It was therefore a major internal failure of the CIA that information about SAM sites in the vicinity of Sverdlovsk was not forwarded to U-2 mission planners – for it so happened that the next U-2 mission would take the aircraft over that location. Even before the 9 April overflight, that mission had already been authorised by the US President but on the condition that it would be conducted before 1 May 1960 because a summit of the leaders of the United States, the Soviet Union, Great Britain and France was planned to take place in Paris on 17 May 1960. The 9 April overflight did not result in a Soviet note of protest and if another successful mission took place more than two weeks before the scheduled top-level meeting, it was reasonable to believe that it would not affect the political climate at the summit. This summit was important if the coming-together of leaders was to produce any positive results. However, for a number of reasons such as the weather and aircraft availability, it proved difficult to meet the deadline, and in the end the mission went ahead on 1 May 1960.[2] Arguably this was not a good date for such an undertaking, as 1 May is International Workers' Day and the USSR saw itself as the self-proclaimed champion of the working class, celebrating it with, among other things, a massive parade in Moscow's Red Square. A deep penetration reconnaissance mission over the Soviet Union on that day was sure to be viewed as a particularly blatant provocation (even though nothing points to such intent) thus jeopardising President Eisenhower's otherwise careful political planning, regardless of whether the aircraft performing it was intercepted or not.

Showdown Over Sverdlovsk

The overflight would not be an ordinary mission. While previously U-2s had deeply penetrated into Soviet airspace, flying inside it for hours, Mission 4154 (Operation Grand Slam) was to be the first mission to reconnoitre the entire country: the U-2 was supposed to fly across the USSR from the south to the north and then land in Norway. An experienced pilot was selected to fly the U-2 on this occasion; Francis Gary Powers. On 1 May 1960, the U-2 was sitting on the runway at Peshawar in Pakistan from where the mission was to be flown. Now, only the coded 'go ahead' for the mission had to arrive from Washington. Due to difficulties arising with radio communications, problems were encountered with relaying the authorisation but finally it was received and the U-2, with Powers at the controls took off, headed from Pakistan to Afghanistan and then into Soviet airspace.[3]

The Soviets detected the intruding aircraft as early as 0536 hours in the morning. By 0600 hours, the main air defence command post in Moscow took over the coordination of efforts aimed at intercepting the foreign aircraft, while an hour later Marshal Siergiey Biryuzov arrived there to supervise its actions. Meanwhile, Khrushchev learned of the incident and, as could have been expected, he was indignant, suspecting that a US reconnaissance mission on this particular date, 1 May, was a deliberate provocation even if in retrospect nothing in available American sources points to such an intention. He ordered the intruder to be destroyed at all costs and voiced his displeasure with the air defences' inability to deal with it. In response, Marshal Biryuzov exclaimed that if he could, he would turn himself into a missile and down the 'damned intruder'.[4] Meanwhile, Soviet air defences were placed on full combat alert and at the same time all civilian aircraft were instructed to land at the nearest airfield. With the skies cleared, the Soviets were now contemplating how to deal with the intruder. The foreign aircraft was tracked by radar and it soon become obvious that it was heading for Sverdlovsk. In a way, this was good news for the Soviets because around the city there were six S-75 *divizion* (missile battalions) of the PVO's 37th and 57th Anti-Aircraft Rocket Brigades, out of which one was 'down' due to a technical problem with its radar.[5] In addition, fighter aviation units were also based in the vicinity.

There was a realistic chance of finally bringing down the American reconnaissance aircraft.

Since it could not be guaranteed that the U-2 would enter the engagement zone of SAMs, it was also decided to scramble fighters. Bearing in mind Khrushchev's directive 'to destroy the target at all cost', General Yevgeny Savitskiy, who was the commander of the Fighter Aviation of the Air Defence Force, issued an order to engage the intruder with all flights located in the area of the foreign aircraft's course to be on alert, standing by on QRA, and to ram it if necessary.[6] It almost came to that, for it so happened that by pure coincidence on 30 April 1960 there were Su-9 interceptors which made an in-flight stop at Kolcovo airfield near Sverdlovsk while being delivered from the manufacturer to an operational unit. One of the pilots, Captain Igor Mientiukov, was ordered to scramble, tasked with intercepting and destroying a target flying at high altitude. Because the Sukhoi was being ferried from the factory, it carried no armament, air-to-air missiles were not available at Kolcovo and the Su-9 had no gun. For these reasons, it seemed that the task assigned was impossible to fulfil, yet the order stood, and Captain Mientiukov took off. Once he was airborne and established radio contact with the ground control, he not only received information about the target but also an order to ram it. The mission was for all practical purposes suicidal, for even if the pilot survived the collision, the effects of high-altitude ejection could also be lethal. Captain Mientiukov was guided by ground control to intercept the U-2 on a rear chase course. When the distance to the target was about 25 kilometres, the pilot was ordered to jettison external fuel tanks and to ignite the afterburner. The speed of his mount rapidly rose to Mach 1.9, while he climbed to 20,000 metres. Just as the distance to the U-2 decreased to 12 kilometres, the American aircraft made a turn and the Soviet pilot, who had no visual contact with the target but was guided by GCI, was instructed to follow it. However, when flying with a high speed and at a high altitude the Su-9, like most other aircraft, was not very manoeuvrable. As a result, Captain Mientiukov missed the target by about eight kilometres which, considering his aircraft's speed, was not as much as it would seem at first glance. He could not simply turn around and reattack, but it was necessary to reposition him for another interception attempt. In order to do this, he was instructed to cut the afterburner and lose speed. Just as the Sukhoi's pilot complied with the order a new one followed: he was to disengage and leave the area immediately. It turned out that in the meantime, the U-2 had entered the engagement zone of SAM batteries defending Sverdlovsk. The first missile salvo was already in the air and friendly aircraft were to get out of the way.

It appears the first to open fire was the *5th Divizion* of the 37th Brigade under the command of Lieutenant Colonel Novikov. The unit launched a missile at 0846 hours and according to one of the subsequent analyses of the engagement, it actually shot the U-2 down.[7] However, this cannot be the case as the distance to the target would have been circa 50 to 60 kilometres, meaning it would have been out of range.[8] Meanwhile, the U-2 entered the engagement zone of the *2nd Divizion* of the 57th Brigade under the command of Major Mikhail Voronov. At 0852 hours a surface-to-air missile was launched on his order.[9] Initially only a single missile was fired because a safety lock prevented the launching of a salvo, but soon more missiles were sent skywards. Shortly thereafter, the SAM operators reported that on the radar screen the target 'started to blink', as they put it. This meant that it was either hit and disintegrating or employing jamming. The missile had detonated behind the U-2 with the blast and fragments causing crippling damage to the American aircraft. As a result, the U-2 was falling from the sky, breaking up on the way down. But Major Voronov and his subordinates could not see this, for they observed the action on radar screens which gave a picture more open to interpretation. Since it could not be taken for granted that the U-2 was shot down, Major Voronov ordered more missiles to be launched and he also did not initially report the destruction of the target. Meanwhile at 0853 hours fire was also opened by the *1st Divizion* commanded by Captain Nikolai Sheludko.[10]

By the time Powers' U-2 was approaching Sverdlovsk, it had been airborne for about four and a half hours.[11] There seemed to be no indication of the impending disaster. Suddenly there was an explosion behind him, followed by a brilliant orange light. Unable to control his stricken mount, Powers could do nothing more than save himself. This was not easy, for in order to eject the pilot had to move the seat back so as to get his legs from underneath the instrument panel. However, the seat jammed and would not move, hence Powers could not eject but had to bail out manually instead. He jettisoned the canopy, unfastened his seat harness and soon found himself clear of the cockpit. Had Powers ejected, a self-destruct mechanism including 2.5–3 lbs (1.13–1.36kg) of cyclonite would have been activated automatically; however, because the American pilot bailed out, it had to be switched manually. Powers failed to do that because he could not reach the switch. Obviously, the small amount of explosives could not have destroyed the whole aircraft but the charge was placed so as to obliterate the photographic equipment. The U-2's wreckage with cameras and film thus came down relatively intact.

Since there was no report citing the destruction of foreign aircraft, the seemingly logical conclusion was that it still had to be shot down. Therefore, when unidentified aircraft entered the engagement zone of the *4th Divizion* under the command of Major Shugayev, he ordered a missile salvo to be launched at 0923 hours.[12] It turned out that the aircraft engaged was a MiG-19 with Senior Lieutenant Sergey Safronov in the cockpit. Once again, the SAMs proved their deadly effectiveness but unfortunately against a friendly aircraft: not only was the MiG shot down, but its pilot lost his life. It has to be explained at this point, that aside from the Su-9 with Captain Mientiukov at the controls, a few more fighters were also ordered to take off; however, apart from the two MiG-19s of the 365th IAP flown by Captain Boris Aivazian and Senior Lieutenant Sergey Safronov (leader and wingman respectively), they played no role in the unfolding events. Previous experience clearly demonstrated that the MiGs were unable to intercept a U-2. However, one could always hope for a lucky chance as the American aircraft might lose altitude because of a malfunction or for some other reason. Once in the air, the MiGs were guided by ground control to the area where the American reconnaissance aircraft operated and their pilots soon sighted debris falling from the sky. These were the remains of the shot-down U-2 but nobody realised it at that time. All of a sudden, an explosion enveloped the MiG flown by Senior Lieutenant Safronov. The pilot ejected but was mortally wounded and probably died under the parachute before he reached the ground. His lifeless body was found by the locals near the village of Degtyarka, west of Sverdlovsk. Meanwhile Captain Aivazian, who flew the other MiG, had more luck for when the disaster struck he instinctively dived and brought himself out of danger. A subsequent analysis revealed that aside from Major Voronov's hesitations, the main reason for this incident was poor coordination between various air defence assets. In addition, it was claimed that the IFF transponders of the MiGs either did not work or were transmitting the wrong code. As a result, the fighters showed on the radar screens of Major Shugayev's

Wreckage of F. G. Power's U-2 (including the right intake) on display at the Central Armed Forces Museum in Moscow. Having failed to bring down any U-2s on previous occasions, the Soviets were satisfied to the point of being gleeful when they finally did. (Photo by D Zubkov)

unit as 'unidentified' instead of 'friendly'. This finding was contested by Captain Aivazian who stated that an IFF check was performed before take-off. In an attempt to reconcile these contradictory claims, it was also reported that the IFF codes of the fighters were not changed as they should have been from the ones used in April to those valid in May. Regardless of how the problem came about and who was to blame, one thing stood clear: the dramatic demise of the MiG was a spectacular and embarrassing case of fratricide. For this reason, Senior Lieutenant Safronov's death was kept secret for many years.

Meanwhile, Powers floated down to earth under his parachute which had automatically opened at a predetermined altitude. Since he was literally in the middle of the Soviet Union, hiding or offering resistance was futile. Powers did not make use of a poisoned needle he was provided with (there was no obligation to do so, which would have been inhumane and unenforceable anyway) and instead he allowed approaching locals to hand him over to the authorities. Subsequently, he was first taken to Sverdlovsk, then brought to the local airfield and finally taken aboard an aircraft destined for Moscow. According to some accounts, he was briefly shown to the Soviet pilots who had attempted to intercept him (they had meanwhile landed) in order to give them a symbolic reward for their efforts.[13] As soon as there were no doubts about the downing of the intruder, the news was reported to Khrushchev. A special commission was swiftly dispatched from the Soviet capital and arrived at the scene within hours. Its task was to investigate the events which had taken place as well as to gather material evidence, especially the remains of the American aircraft. The U-2 broke up in the air with not only the wings but also the tail and other parts separating from the aircraft's main body as it was going down. Yet despite being scattered on the ground over an area of several square kilometres, the wreckage of the U-2 was quickly located and collected. Among the items recovered, of particular interest to the Soviets was the photographic equipment and the rolls of film it contained. After being examined by Soviet experts, the remains of the U-2 were put on display in Moscow's Gorky Park, being shown to the Soviet leadership, journalists and the general public.[14]

Altogether, the SAM units involved fired between eight and 14 surface-to-air missiles to shoot down two aircraft: the American U-2 reconnaissance aircraft and one of their own MiGs.[15] Of the men involved in the downing of the US reconnaissance aircraft, 21 were decorated with various medals, among them Senior Lieutenant Sergey Safronov, but since his death resulted from an embarrassing case of fratricide, the word 'posthumously' was not added next to his name in the official announcement. Major Mikhail Voronov was decorated with the Order of the Red Banner, receiving medal number 530334.[16] The principal reason for which he was not put forward for the Hero of the Soviet Union title and medal was that the shooting down of Powers' U-2 also led to the fratricidal downing of Safronov's MiG-19.

Thus far the events were related mainly from the Soviet perspective, yet it also seems fitting to address American side of the story, in particular the shootdowns' aftermath.[17] Once it was realised that the U-2 had disappeared, presumably being lost, the National Aeronautics and Space Administration issued a press release claiming that one of its aircraft performing a high-altitude research mission had gone missing. Further, it was claimed that the pilot radioed a message about supposed oxygen problems. Conclusions implied were that the pilot fell unconscious, but with the autopilot engaged the aircraft flew on, penetrating Soviet territory. The cover story was agreed on beforehand but not honed concerning its finer points and thus its credibility, for no-one really expected the U-2 to come down in the middle of the Soviet Union. Last but not least, Powers was not briefed on what the cover story would be either. Having intentionally waited for the US announcement before making his own, Khrushchev had the information released that a reconnaissance aircraft had been shot down over Soviet territory, but he did not yet reveal that the pilot of that aircraft was captured alive. The Americans kept maintaining their cover story only to be exposed with Khrushchev's announcement on 7 May 1960 that the U-2's pilot was alive and in Soviet custody. At that point, the United States was put into a decidedly unfavourable position both politically as well as propaganda-wise. Moreover, President Eisenhower found himself in a situation demanding that he either took personal responsibility for this act and its results or appear not to be in control of the government and its agencies if the blame was assigned to others. President Eisenhower was not short on courage and took responsibility for what had happened. He also argued, not without having a point, that Soviet secretiveness necessitated vigilance and thus overflights of the Soviet Union were in their essence not signs of aggressive intent but defensive cautiousness. The planned summit in Paris collapsed because Khrushchev demanded an apology from Eisenhower – a demand to which the latter would not yield. This halted efforts to bring about better relations between the United States and the Soviet Union which was not an insignificant matter considering that both were nuclear-armed, though at that time the former held an advantage in this regard over the latter. Considering the way the Soviets handled the aftermath of the U-2's downing and the capture of its pilot, they arguably extracted the maximum short term propaganda effect from the event and caused the United States and the country's president much embarrassment. Having said that, they failed to secure any significant long-term advantage which they might have attained had they been somewhat more conciliatory. It is an old wisdom that being gracious when having the upper hand is not a sign of weakness and more frequently than not, it pays off.

Major Mikhail Voronov receiving his Order of Red Banner from commander of the 4th Independent Air Defence Army, General Yevgeniy Korshunov. (Soviet Ministry of Defence)

Powers, having been flown from Sverdlovsk to Moscow, was brought to and held at Lubyanka, which housed the headquarters of the Soviet KGB.[18] Unfortunately, U-2 pilots were not properly trained for such a situation and Powers had to improvise. He tried as best he could to only give information which was available in open sources or could be deduced from an examination of his downed aircraft. It should be underscored that while this was obviously not pleasant and it was tiring, the American was not tortured or otherwise abused. Once the questioning was over, Powers was put on trial, charged with espionage. Since it was pointless to deny his intelligence-gathering activity, he confessed his guilt and made a statement to the effect that he was sorry for what had happened. On 19 August 1960, Francis Gary Powers was sentenced to 10 years' confinement. Fortunately, the U-2 pilot did not have to serve his sentence in full. On 10 February 1962, he was freed in a 'spy swap' at the Glienicke Bridge in Berlin, Germany. On that occasion, the Soviet spy Rudolf Abel (William August Fisher) was exchanged for Francis Gary Powers and two American students, Frederic Pryor and Marvin Makinen, who were held on charges of espionage (though they might have been victims of 'being at the wrong place at the wrong time'), were also released as part of the same deal. Pryor had been in East Germany and Makinen in the Soviet Union. Powers was swiftly returned to the United States, but this did not end his woes yet. Critical voices were raised, with some dissatisfied with the fact that he allowed himself to be captured instead of committing suicide. Powers was extensively debriefed by the Central Intelligence Agency, the U-2's manufacturer Lockheed Corporation, as well as the US Air Force. Once this was over, he underwent a hearing before the Senate Armed Services Select Committee. In the end, Powers was not only exonerated of any wrongdoing but even received praise for his actions and conduct. However, he still received his Intelligence Star medal in 1965 instead of 1963 as other U-2 pilots had, while many other decorations including the Distinguished Flying Cross were awarded to him only posthumously. The difficulties Powers faced were also of a more practical nature. His return to service with the US Air Force turned out to be problematic. He found employment with the Lockheed Corporation as a test pilot but lost the job after the book relating his experience, titled *Operation Overflight*, which he co-authored with Curt Gentry was published. In the end, he worked as a helicopter pilot for a Los Angeles TV station. Unfortunately, his story had no happy ending for Powers was killed when the helicopter he flew crashed on 1 August 1977. Francis Gary Powers was laid to rest with honours in the Arlington National Cemetery.[19]

No Nonsense in the North

High-altitude overflights of the Soviet Union ended for good with the shooting down of Powers' U-2. That said, intelligence-gathering missions along the USSR's periphery continued. Such missions included those performed by RB-47H reconnaissance aircraft of the USAF's 38th Strategic Reconnaissance Squadron, which was based at Forbes Air Force Base, in Kansas, United States, but which flew operational sorties from RAF Brize Norton in Great Britain. On 1 July 1960, exactly two months after the U-2 flown by Powers was shot down, the RB-47H serial number 53-4281 and nicknamed 'The Little Toy Dog' took off from Brize Norton. The aircraft was flown by Major Willard Palm (commander), Captain Freeman B. Olmstead (pilot), and Captain John McKone (navigator) with three more men operating electronic equipment: Major Eugene Posa, Captain Dean Phillips and Captain Oscar Goforth. The latter trio had their stations in an enclosed compartment which occupied the space normally taken by the bomb bay of the B-47. In addition, the aircraft had a seventh 'crewmember' of sorts, namely a small toy dog mascot which Major Palm carried with him for luck.[20]

Many hours of solitary flight had already passed for the RB-47's crew when suddenly they got company of the undesirable sort: the Americans were intercepted over the Barents Sea by a MiG-19 fighter of the 174th GIAP flown by Captain Vasyli Polyakov.[21] Subsequent accounts differed, not only on how the situation developed but even where the encounter took place. According to the Soviets, it must have been right off Cape Svyatoy Nos, whereas the Americans maintained that they were no closer than 30 miles (55 kilometres) from that location – arguably, this will never be established with certainty. Having intercepted the US aircraft, the MiG pilot first took a station off the RB-47's right wing and subsequently rocked the wings of his own mount, in what is an established signal conveying to the Americans that they had been intercepted and were to follow. Since this did not result in their compliance, the Soviet pilot opened fire with cannon on the US aircraft, making two passes and firing 111 rounds. The Americans attempted to return fire with the RB-47's tail gun but claimed its fire control radar was jammed. However, as far as it is known, the MiG-19 did not have such electronic warfare capabilities and thus it is more likely that the Americans' defensive armament suffered some malfunction. As a result of the MiG's attacks, the US aircraft sustained crippling damage and went down. The flight crew managed to eject: Captains McKone and Olmsted were rescued by a Soviet fishing trawler, but Major Palm lost his life. The latter's body was recovered and subsequently returned to the United States. All the men operating the RB-47's electronics perished with the aircraft. It was established that of this trio, only the remains of Major Posa were confirmed to have been found at a later date, but for reasons which still remain unclear instead of being returned to the United States, they were buried at an undisclosed location. It is possible, though far from certain, that additional bodies may have been recovered. Unfortunately, even if it was indeed the case, what subsequently happened to them could not be ascertained. In a somewhat macabre postscript, a few month later a decomposing human leg, very likely belonging to one of the killed Americans, was hauled with the nets aboard a Soviet fishing vessel but was promptly thrown overboard by the order of its captain.[22] The toy dog mascot, which on this occasion failed to bring luck, went down with the ill-fated aircraft. Once landed ashore, Captains McKone and Olmsted

A MiG-19PM of the PVO near the left wingtip of an RB-47H over the Baltic Sea on 24 September 1962. Notably, the Soviet pilot pulled out a camera to photograph the American reconnaissance bomber, as the crew of the latter was photographing him. Obviously, the encounter between the two types on 1 July 1960 over the Barents Sea was much less peaceful. (Albert Grandolini Collection)

The view from the forward fuselage of an RB-47H at the three 'ravens': mission specialists operating reconnaissance equipment installed inside the modified bomb bay. (Albert Grandolini Collection)

were brought to Moscow and were held at Lubyanka. They underwent lengthy and obviously unpleasant interrogations, though suffered no physical torture, unless one counts the very meagre food rations they were fed and the Soviet cigarettes they were occasionally given to smoke. Meanwhile, American diplomats in Moscow were making efforts to secure their release but to no avail. For some time, the Soviets thought about putting the US airmen on trial for espionage but decided against it. Apparently, they concluded that it would be politically more beneficial to free the Americans as a goodwill gesture to the newly inaugurated US President, John F. Kennedy. Accordingly, both airmen were released into the hands of US diplomats on 24 January 1961. Noteworthy is that unlike Powers, upon their return Captains McKone and Olmsted got nothing short of a heroes' welcome and were received by President Kennedy at the White House.[23]

Saluting a fallen hero: the repatriation of Captain Palm's mortal remains. (Albert Grandolini Collection)

Captain Polyakov receiving his Order of Red Banner (from left to right): Secretary of the Presidium of the Supreme Soviet Mikhail Georgadze, Head of the Presidium of the Supreme Soviet Leonid Brezhnev, Captain Vasiliy Polyakov, and commander of PVO Fighter Aviation, General Yevgeniy Savitskiy. (TASS)

It is not entirely clear how the shootdown itself came about. Captain Polyakov may have handled it at his own discretion, since the standing order to destroy aircraft violating Soviet airspace should have served as sufficient justification for his actions. It was also reported that his resolve was strengthened because the RB-47H was supposed to be heading for a secret nuclear submarine base. The latter explanation, however, appears to be very unlikely for even if a captain of the Air Defence Force knew about a secret base of the navy, it meant such a facility was not secret at all. Alternatively, available sources seem to indicate he might have been advised to shoot the US aircraft down by a ground control officer, Senior Lieutenant Anatoliy Kotlyarov.[24] The latter apparently took it upon himself to say the fateful words when all officers senior to him, who were present and were listening over the radio to Captain Polyakov relating how the situation was developing, somewhat conveniently suffered from a temporary loss of speech. In any case, when Captain Polyakov returned to base, his immediate superiors and all senior officers up the chain of command were initially startled. Once it was established that this was not a case of fratricide (at first it was speculated his victim might have been a Soviet Tu-16), it became clear that a very serious international incident had taken place. To make matters worse, at least from the point of view of the Soviet leadership, such actions of a senior lieutenant and a captain meant either that senior officers had no control over their subordinates or that crucial decisions of potentially grave consequences were left in the hands of junior officers, which basically made all the generals and marshals seem redundant, at least in the eyes of someone like Khrushchev. Fortunately for all those involved on the Soviet side, it turned out that the Soviet leader was personally satisfied with what had happened, treating the whole matter in the vein of 'teaching the Americans a lesson'. When he inquired 'where is our hero?' a surprised Marshal Malinovski did not understand who Khrushchev was talking about, but Marshal Biryuzov swiftly grasped it, replying 'all ours are like this', that is, all his men were as resolute and combative as the one who shot the US aircraft down. The end result was that Captain Polyakov not only avoided any negative

Captain Bruce Olmstead and Captain John McKone, the two surviving crewmembers of the RB-47H shot down by a PVO MiG-19 over the Barents Sea on 1 July 1960, seen upon their return to the USA in January 1961. (Albert Grandolini Collection)

consequences for his actions but was decorated with the Order of the Red Banner at the Kremlin.[25]

Never Again

Closing this subject, one cannot but observe that the spring of 1960 was a hot period of the Cold War in the air with two American reconnaissance aircraft shot down by the Soviets in the timespan of just two months. The 1 May 1960 incident fundamentally changed U-2 operations for they would never be the same again. Its obvious result was that manned reconnaissance overflights involving deep penetrations of Soviet airspace were discontinued. Technically speaking, they were merely halted on the order of President Eisenhower, an order his successor John F. Kennedy upheld, but one which theoretically could have been countermanded at any given time. There were some voices calling for this, especially since other intelligence-gathering methods could not for some time yet provide the quality and quantity of reconnaissance information the U-2s did, though in the end they were never again intentionally sent over the Soviet Union.[26] Similarly, the RB-47 shot down on 1 June 1960 was the last instance of a confirmed downing of a US reconnaissance aircraft during a peripheral intelligence-gathering mission along the USSR's borders, at least as far as available sources allow for such a conclusion.[27] Thus the 'hot' spring of 1960 was truly the end of an era as far as US aerial reconnaissance of the Soviet Union was concerned. Yet since the Cold War was far from over, the need for intelligence persisted. However, with the deployment of reconnaissance satellites came profound changes in the manner in which it was gathered. The first successful mission that resulted in recovery of intelligence data by the CORONA reconnaissance satellite took place on 18 August 1960.[28] Having said this, it should be kept in mind that it still took time before satellites were able to provide large volumes of high-quality intelligence on a regular basis. Moreover, certain kinds of data could not be obtained by space-based systems alone. For those reasons, in particular the latter, US and allied aircraft continued to skirt the fringes of the 'Red empire', sometimes even crossing the border (both accidentally and intentionally) which resulted in a number of incidents; this being a story to be told separately.

14
THE PVO LEARNS TO WALK

In the late 1940s and 1950s, particularly in the second half of the latter decade, Soviet air defences went through profound changes. The decision in 1954 to reorganise the PVO as well as to elevate it to a separate branch of the armed forces was of great importance. From then on, its responsibilities vis-à-vis other branches were clearly delimited, and it was given the necessary organisational framework to function efficiently. Yet all this would have been nothing but administrative reshuffling without giving the PVO the necessary tools to fulfil its mission. Such were provided and not only were a large number of radar sets delivered but work was in progress to link them into one functional entity as well as to give it a capability to provide, via radio-link, guidance data for interception to fighter aircraft. The ground-based anti-aircraft arsenal was developed and modernised too. Initial efforts concentrated on fielding traditional AA guns, but ones with ever-growing calibre and thus reach, though smaller calibre pieces were developed too. Efforts subsequently switched to guided surface-to-air missiles, and success in the form of two operational SAM systems, the S-25 and S-75, was achieved. Similarly, fighter aviation underwent an evolution: starting with piston-engine fighters, it re-equipped with subsonic jets, then supersonic examples, and finally Mach 2-capable interceptors. Last but not least, guided air-to-air missiles were developed to arm them.

If Everything Was So Good Why Was It So Bad?

Having outlined the Soviet AD's progress and its combat operations of the 1950s, it still needs to be remembered that neither was Rome build in one day, nor did the PVO attain its full potential overnight. The USSR's borders were around 60,000 kilometres long and as a result, despite an ever-growing surveillance net, there were serious gaps in its radar coverage. Moreover, in order to give such a huge country as the Soviet Union (at that time the largest in the world) with numerous cities, industrial facilities, military installations and so on even a modest defence from air attack, the numbers of AA guns and SAMs as well as fighter aircraft needed were almost unimaginably large, requiring a gargantuan effort to develop, manufacture and deploy them, with this effort being time consuming too. Additionally, introducing new as well as technically complex systems such as radars, SAMs, missile-armed interceptors and so on brought with it a number of challenges. Everyone, from radar operators, ground controllers and pilots to ground crews had to gain experience in utilising their capabilities as well as properly operating them. Numerous failed attempts to intercept high-flying British and US reconnaissance aircraft were a clear illustration of how difficult it actually was. Even when a successful outcome was eventually achieved, serious mistakes, such as fratricidal shootdowns, were not avoided. Summarising the state of affairs, it can be stated that by 1960, the PVO was not yet firmly standing on its feet, but it was learning to walk and making noticeable progress at that.

By 1960, the PVO had Mach 2-capable, missile-armed interceptors in operational service, such as this Su-9. However, it still took time before enough of these were available and the service mastered the art of operating them properly. (Albert Grandolini Collection)

The late 1950s saw the introduction of two effective SAM systems into the arsenal of the PVO, the first of which was the S-25 – to which this V-300 missile belonged. This was a major step in bolstering the service's capability, and the Soviets took considerable pride in their missiles: this is why these always featured prominently during parades held on the Victory Day, the October Revolution anniversary, and other occasions. (Albert Grandolini Collection)

BIBLIOGRAPHY

Alekhin, Yu., et al., *Piramida nachalas s Vozdukha* Vozdushno-Kosmicheskaya oborona magazine №1, 2011

Angelskiy, R., Korovin V., *Otechestvennyye upravlyayemyye rakety vozdukh-vozdukh* Tekhnika i vooruzheniye magazine №9 / 2005

Austin, H., *A Cold War Over Flight of the USSR*, 307TH Bomb Wing Association Newsletter No 30, March 2000

Belyakov, R. A., & Marmen Zh., *Samolety MiG 1939 - 1995* (Aviko Press, 1996)

Boyne, W. J., *Reconnaissance on the Wing*, Air Force Magazine, October 1999

Brookes, A., *RAF Canberra Units of the Cold War* (Oxford: Osprey Publishing, 2014)

Brown, A. E., *Dropshot: The United States Plan for War with the Soviet Union in 1957 (New York: Dial Press 1978)*

Canberra in the RAF (Royal Air Force Historical Society, 2009)

Dabrowski, K, *Hunt for the U-2* (Warwick, Helion &Co, 2020)

Dabrowski, K, *Tsar Bomba* (Warwick, Helion &Co, 2021)

Dokuchayev, A., *'Okhota v stratosfere'*, Aviatsiya i Kosmonavtika magazine, Vol. 4/2000

East, D. C., *The History of U.S. Naval Airborne Electronic Reconnaissance Part I, The Pacific and VQ-1*, The Hook: Journal of Carrier Aviation, Spring 1987

East, D. C., *The History of U.S. Naval Airborne Electronic Reconnaissance Part II, The European Theatre and VQ-2*, The Hook: Journal of Carrier Aviation, Summer 1987

Farquhar, J. T., *A Need to Know: The Role of Air Force Reconnaissance in War Planning 1945–1953* (Maxwell Air Force Base: Air University Press, 2004)

Fensch, T., *The C.I.A. and the U-2 Program 1954–1974* (The Woodlands, Texas: New Century Books, 2001)

Flintham, V., *Air Wars and Aircraft: A Detailed Record of Air Combat 1945 to the Present* (London: Arms and Armour Press, 1989)

Glenshaw, P., *Secret Casualties of the Cold War*, Air & Space Magazine, December 2017

Grigoryev, Y., *Neobyavlennaya vozdushnaya voyna SSSR i SSHA*, Istorik magazine, 2016 – №3

Grisell, B. et al., *The DC-3: a KTH project* (Stockholm: Royal Institute of Technology, 2007)

Hallion, R. P., *Silver Wings, Golden Valor: The USAF Remembers Korea* (CreateSpace Independent Publishing Platform, 2006)

Jackson, R., *High Cold War: Strategic Air Reconnaissance and the Electronic Intelligence War* (Sparkford: Patrick Stephens Ltd./ Haynes Publishing)

Khrushchev, N. S., *Khrushchev Remembers: The Last Testament* (Boston: Little Brown and Company, 1974)

Kotlobovskiy, A., &, Seidov I., *Goryacheye nebo "kholodnoy voyny"* pt. 1 & 2 Mir Aviatsii magazine, №2(10)'95 & №1(11) '96

Knutov, Yu., *Pauersa sbil mayor Voronov*, Vozdushno-Kosmicheskaya oborona magazine № 4 2013

Kucheryaev, N., *Svalyt Gerkulesa*, Istoriya Aviatsii magazine №27 2004

Lipayev, V., *Pervoye avtomatizirovannoye navedeniye istrebitelya-perekhvatchika na tsel*, Aviapanorama magazine №5, 2014

Meshkov, A., *Vysokoe masterstvo* pt. 1 & 2 Sovetskaya Aviatsiya journal, 19 & 20 September 1958

Napier, M., *The Royal Air Force: A Centenary of Operations* (Oxford: Osprey Publishing, 2018)

Orlov, A.S., *Taynaya bitva sverkhderzhav* (Moscow: Veche, 2000)

Orlov, A.S., *Vozdushnaya razvedka SSHA nad territoriyey SSSR v 1950-1955 gg.* Novaya i Noveyshaya istoriya No 6, 2000

Pedlow, G. W. & Welzenbach, D. E., *The Central Intelligence Agency and Overhead Reconnaissance: The U-2 and OXCART Programs, 1954-1974* (Washington DC: Central Intelligence Agency, History Staff, 1992)

Peebles, C., *Shadow Flights: America's Secret Air War Against the Soviet Union: A Cold War History* (Novato, California: Presidio Press, 2000)

Peterson, M. L., *Maybe You Had To Be There: The SIGINT on Thirteen Soviet Shootdowns of U.S. Reconnaissance Aircraft*, Cryptologic Quarterly, Vol. 12, No. 2, Summer 1993

Pocock, C., *Operation 'Robin' and the British Overflight of Kapustin Yar: A Historiographical Note*, Intelligence and National Security, Vol.17, No.4, Winter 2002

Powers, F.G., With Gentry C., *Operation Overflight: the U-2 spy pilot tells his story for the first time* (Holt, Rinehart and Winston, 1970)

Richardson, D., *Techniques and Equipment of Electronic Warfare* (London: Salamander Books Ltd., 1985)

Richardson, J.T., *American Espionage and the Soviet Target* (New York: William Morrow & Company, 1987)

Samokhin, A.V., *Vozdushnaya oborona granits SSSR v nachale 1950—th godov* Voyenno-Istoricheskiy Zhurnal magazine 2016 №12

Samoylov, B., *Zagadka pervomaya 1960 goda* pt. 1 & 2 Voyenno-Promyshlennyy Kuryer № 4 (421) & № 5 (422)

Serov, G., *Strategicheskaya vozdushnaya razvedka NATO protiv SSSR 1950-ye gody* Mir Aviatsii magazine, №1(24)2001, №1(28)2002

Serov, G., FOMICH A. *S-25. Kak sozdavalas' pervaya otechestvennaya ZRS* Aerokosmicheskoye obozreniye magazine №2 / 2006

Shirokorad, A.B., *Istoriya aviatsionnogo vooruzheniya* (Minsk: Kharvest, 1999)

Shirokorad, A.B., *Entsiklopediya otechestvennoy artillerii* (Minsk: Kharvest, 1999)

Shirokorad, A.B., *Velikaya kontributsiya. Chto SSSR poluchil posle voyny* (Moscow: Veche, 1999)

Veronico, N.A., *Privateer Shoot-Down: How the Cold War claimed Consolidated PB4Y-3 BuNo 59645*, Air Classics magazine, November 2016

West, N., *Historical Dictionary of Cold War Counterintelligence* (Lanham, Maryland: Rowman & Littlefield, 2006)

White, K., *World in Peril; The Origin, Mission, and Scientific Findings of the 46th/72nd Reconnaissance Squadron* (Elkhart, Ind: K.W. White & Associates, 1994)

White, W.L, *The Little Toy Dog: the story of the two RB-47 flyers, Captain John R. McKone and Captain Freeman B. Olmstead* (New York: Dutton, 1962)

Winkler, D.F., *Cold War at Sea: The maritime confrontation on and over the high seas between the United States and the Soviet Union 1945-1989* (PhD thesis) (Washington D.C.: The American University, 1998)

Yakubovich, N., *Samolety S. A. Lavochkina* (Moscow: Rusavia, 2002)
Yakubovich, N., *La-7, La-9, La-11. Posledniye porshnevyye istrebiteli SSSR* (Moscow: Eksmo, 2014)
Yakubovich, N., *Aviakollektsiya № 5 2014 Mnogotselevoy samolet Yak-25* (ZAO Redaktsiya zhurnala 'Modelist-konstruktor', 2014)
Yakubovich, N., *Pervyye sverkhzvukovyye istrebiteli MiG-17 i MiG-19* (Moscow: Eksmo, 2014)
Yakubovich, N., *Aviakollektsiya № 3 2019 Istrebiteli-perekhvatchiki SU-9 i SU-11* (ZAO Redaktsiya zhurnala 'Modelist-konstruktor', 2019)
Zaloga, S., *Red SAM: The SA-2 Guideline Anti-Aircraft Missile* (Oxford: Osprey Publishing Ltd, 2007)
Zaretskiy, B. L., *Voyska PVO strany: vzlety i padeniya* Vozdushno-Kosmicheskaya oborona magazine № 3, 2012

Online Sources

Accomplishments of the U-2 Program, CIA memo TCS-7519-60 dated 27 May 1960, available at https://www.archive.org
Aid, M., *The Soviet Target: The US Intelligence Community Versus the USSR* (online publication available at https://primarysources.brillonline.com)
Air Combat Information Group (ACIG), forum and database at https://www.acig.info
Boyne, W.J., *The early overflights,* https://www.airforcemag.com/article
Bureau of Aircraft Accidents Archives, https://www.baaa-acro.com
Caswell, J., *Remembering Crew Members of U.S. Navy PB4Y-2 Shoot Down, April 8, 1950 – And Shocking Cold War Case Study* (online publication available at https://stationhypo.com/)
Dashlay, F.Z., et al., *Krylya Batayskoy Lotnoy Kniga 2* (online publication available at http://people.my-bataysk.ru)
DOCID: 3901038 (online document pertaining to the downing of the USAF C-130 on 2 September 1958 available at https://www.nsa.gov)
Dokuchayev, A., *Samolot-razvedchik RB-47: o vozvrashchenii zabyt* (online publication available at https://zvezdaweekly.ru/news/202010161810-CMJY9.html)
Dwight D. Eisenhower Presidential Library available at https://www.eisenhowerlibrary.gov
Farwell, A.F., *VP-6 P2V Shootdown of a Soviet MIG off Vladivostok 1950* (online publication available at https://www.vp-6.org/content.aspx?page_id=22&club_id=309126&module_id=146970)
Office of Naval Research http://www.onr.navy.mil
PAMYATNIK, 'Raketa V-300 zenitno raketnaya systema S-25 Berkut, Izdeliye 217m, zav No.6222618/6222655', *c-25.su*
Project ROBIN available at https://ncap.org.uk/search?pos=115&archive=6-1-125
Public Papers of the Presidents of the United States: Dwight D. Eisenhower (1955) available at www.govinfo.gov
Raspletin, A.A., 'History PVO', historykpvo.narod2.ru
Raspletin A.A., *Zenitnyy raketnyy kompleks S-75 na vooruzhenii* (online publication available at http://www.biograph.ru/images/stories/raspletin)
Richelson, J.T., *When Secrets Crash* (online publication available at www.airforcemag.com/article/0701crash)
Ruffner, K.C., *Corona: America's First Satellite Program* ADA499635 (online publication available at https://apps.dtic.mil/sti)
Schindler, J.R., *A Dangerous Business: The U.S. Navy and National Reconnaissance During the Cold War* (online publication available at https://www.nsa.gov)
Seydov, I., *91 Strategicheskaya Razvedyvatelnaya Eskadrilya v Koreye* (online publication available at https://www.airforce.ru)
Sholokh, Ye., *Vozdushnyy boy nad ostrovom Askold* (online publication availablc at https://www.airforce.ru)
Spyflight website available at www.spyflight.co.uk
Stratopedia an encyclopaedia about the who, what, when, where and why of scientific ballooning available at http://stratocat.com.ar/stratopedia
Surface-to-Air Missile Site Near Sverdlovsk USSR, Central Intelligence Agency Photographic Intelligence Brief B-1009-59, 13 August 1959 (online publication available at www.cia.gov/readingroom/docs)
The Communicator, Vol V, No. 32, 26 August 1997 (online publication available at https://www.nsa.gov)
US Navy Patrol Squadrons, https://www.vpnavy.org
Van Hare, T., *Reds Down U.S. Bomber; 1 Dead* (online publication available at http://fly.historicwings.com)
Vestnik PVO www.pvo.guns.ru
Zaloga, S., 'Defending the Kremlin: The First Generation of Soviet Strategic Air Defense Systems 1950-60' bobrowen.com

NOTES

Chapter 1

1 Vozdushno-Kosmicheskaya oborona № 3 2012.
2 direktivy voyennogo ministra SSSR № 663035 ot 14 sentyabrya 1951 goda, № 70505 i № 70506 ot 7 yanvarya 1952 goda o sozdanii prigranichnykh rayonov vozdushnoy oborony, ikhgranitsakh i poryadke neseniya sluzhby v etikh rayonakh.
3 Postanovleniye TSK KPSS i Soveta ministrov SSSR № 1040-444ss.
4 Prikaz Ministra Oborony № 0075 ot 14 iyunya 1954.
5 Voyenno-Istoricheskiy Zhurnal 2016 №12.
6 Shirokorad, *Velikaya kontributsiya.*
7 Voyenno-Istoricheskiy Zhurnal 2003 №12.
8 Vestnik PVO www.pvoguns.ru.
9 Mir Aviatsii №1(24)2001.
10 Aviapanorama №5 2014.
11 Vozdushno-Kosmicheskaya oborona №1 2011.

Chapter 2

1 Unless otherwise noted the subchapter is based upon Shirokorad, *Entsiklopediya otechestvennoy artillerii.*
2 Shirokorad, *Velikaya kontributsiya.*
3 Joseph Stalin (Jughashvili) was the general secretary of the Communist Party of the Soviet Union and premier of the Soviet Union. Apart from official posts he also de-facto held close to unlimited dictatorial power from the mid-1920s until his death in 1953.
4 Pamyatnik, 'Raketa V-300'.
5 Shirokorad, *Velikaya kontributsiya.*

6 Pamyatnik, 'Raketa V-300'.
7 Zaloga, 'Defending the Kremlin'.
8 Pamyatnik, 'Raketa V-300'.
9 Of all that was needed only the houses were never built in sufficient numbers, usually two families had to share one, sometimes even more were cramped together.
10 Postanovleniye TSK KPSS i Soveta Ministrov SSSR № 1382-638.
11 Postanovleniye SM SSSR № 2838/1201.
12 Raspletin, *Zenitnyy raketnyy kompleks S-75 na vooruzhenii.*
13 For more details see Dabrowski, *Hunt for the U-2*, p.6.
14 Raspletin, *historykpvo.narod2.ru.*
15 Raspletin, Table 'SAM Exports', *historykpvo.narod2.ru.*
16 For more details see Dabrowski, *Hunt for the U-2*, p.16.

Chapter 3

1 Yakubovitch, *La-7, La-9, La-11.*
2 The individual MiG models have been described in numerous detailed monographs, there are also publications giving a good general overview of MiG aircraft types such as for example Belyakov & Marmen, *Samolety MiG.*
3 Yakubovic, Aviakollektsiya № 5 2014.
4 The Yak-25 was developed into a number of specialised reconnaissance and strike versions which are however beyond the scope of this analysis.
5 Yakubovich, *Samolety S.A. Lavochkina.*
6 Yakubovich, *Istrebiteli-perekhvatchiki SU-9 i SU-11.*
7 Shirkorard, *Istoriya aviatsionnogo vooruzheniya.*
8 Avitsja i vremja 1999 3.
9 Aerokosmicheskoye obozreniye №2 / 2006.
10 Tekhnika i vooruzheniye. №9 / 2005.
11 See Dabrowski, *Hunt for the U-2*, p.15.
12 Tekhnika i vooruzheniye. №9 / 2005.
13 Aviatsiya i Kosmonavtika Vol. 11/2002.

Chapter 4

1 Boyne, *Early overflights.*
2 White, *World in peril.*
3 Soviet Note Number 261, Embassy of the Union of Soviet Socialist Republics, 5 January 1948.
4 Peebles, *Shadow Flights.*
5 Orlov, *Taynaya bitva sverkhderzhav.*
6 Boyne, *Early overflights.*
7 East, *The History of U.S. Naval Airborne Electronic Reconnaissance.*
8 Pedlow et al., *The Central Intelligence Agency and Overhead reconnaissance: the U-2 and OXCART Programs.*
9 Aid, *The Soviet Target.*
10 A few exceptions aside; for example on 10 July 1948 a J 26 (Mustang) with Fredrik "Fred" Christjern Lambert-Meuller overflew the island of Ösel (Saaremaa) which at that time was Soviet controlled (nowadays it belongs to independent Estonia).
11 www.spyflight.co.uk.
12 Iran never operated any kind of aircraft designated 'P-5' or similar (for example, the Stinson L-5). Thus, the author is only able to guess that the aircraft in question might have been a British-made Auster AOP.5, operated by a local civilian aeroclub, or a Cessna 180 or 185 (military versions of which were designated the U-17 or U-17A, respectively), operated by the Imperial Iranian Gendarmerie and the Imperial Iranian Army Aviation.
13 www.skywar.ru – information in Russians sources concerning the incident are spares and while the author made efforts to learn the Iranian side of the story it proved impossible to find a confirmation of it even having happened much less any detailed information.
14 Voyenno-Istoricheskiy Zhurnal 2016 №12.
15 Mir Aviatsii №2(10)'95.
16 https://www.cia.gov/library/readingroom.
17 Center for the Study of Intelligence, CIA Electronic FOIA Website http://www.foia.cia.gov.
18 Orlov, *Taynaya bitva sverkhderzhav.*
19 Unless stated otherwise the Soviet version of the events is sourced from Yakubovitch, *La-7, La-9, La-11.*
20 Orlov, *Taynaya bitva sverkhderzhav.*
21 Dashlay, *Krylya Batayskoy Lotnoy.*
22 Caswell, *Remembering Crew Members of U.S. Navy PB4Y-2 Shoot Down.*
23 Schindler, *A Dangerous Business.*
24 Air Classics, November 2016.
25 Additionally, in 2001 Swedish fisherman found a peculiar 'catch' in their nets which turned out to be one of the Privateer's engines as reported by the Lae – inte bara en stad på Nya Guinea blog (https://lae.blogg.se) .
26 Caswell, *Remembering.*
27 U.S.– Russia Joint Commission on POWs/MIAs Reports available at the Library of Congress web site www.loc.gov.
28 Air Classics, November 2016.

Chapter 5

1 Pedlow et al., *The Central Intelligence Agency and Overhead reconnaissance: the U-2 and OXCART Programs.*
2 See Dabrowski, *Tsar Bomba,* pp.3-14.
3 Mir Aviatsii №2(10)'95.
4 Neither the Bureau of Aircraft Accidents Archives https://www.baaa-acro.com or other similar database nor any other American source known to the author confirms such a loss having occurred.
5 USAF Historical Office, FEAF. History of the Far East Air Forces available at https://www.afhra.af.mil.
6 Peterson, *Maybe You Had To Be There.*
7 U.S.– Russia Joint Commission on POWs/MIAs.
8 Peterson, *Maybe You Had To Be There.*
9 www.vp-6.org.
10 U.S.– Russia Joint Commission on POWs/MIAs.
11 Air & Space magazine Dec 2017.
12 Istorik 2016 – №3.
13 U.S.– Russia Joint Commission on POWs/MIAs.
14 Peterson, *Maybe You Had To Be There.*
15 U.S.– Russia Joint Commission on POWs/MIAs.
16 Air & Space magazine Dec 2017.
17 Air & Space magazine Dec 2017.
18 The nature of the RB-29's mission was acknowledged by U.S.– Russia Joint Commission on POWs/MIAs.
19 Istorik 2016 – №3.
20 The regimental number 369 given in some sources is an obvious mistake.
21 U.S.– Russia Joint Commission on POWs/MIAs.
22 Peterson, *Maybe You Had To Be There.*
23 Peterson, *Maybe You Had To Be There.*
24 U.S.– Russia Joint Commission on POWs/MIAs.
25 The awkward spelling resulting from the Soviets transliterating Dunham John Robertson from the Latin into the Cyrillic alphabet and the USRJC reversing the process.
26 Before the Air Force Academy was established, one-quarter of Naval Academy graduates each year were given the option of joining the Air Force – John Dunham took that option training as a navigator for aerial reconnaissance.
27 Due to the time difference, it was still 28 July in Washington DC when the event occurred.

28 Peterson, *Maybe You Had To Be There.*
29 Orlov, *Taynaya bitva sverkhderzhav.*
30 Sholokh, *Vozdushnyy boy nad ostrovom Askold.*
31 Peterson, *Maybe You Had To Be There.*
32 U.S.– Russia Joint Commission on POWs/MIAs.
33 Peterson, *Maybe You Had To Be There.*
34 U.S.– Russia Joint Commission on POWs/MIAs.

Chapter 6

1 Istorik 2016 – №3.
2 http://khasan-district.narod.ru/directory/mem_kultur/mem_kul.htm.
3 www.airforce.ru.
4 Hallion, *Silver Wings, Golden Valor.*
5 Unless otherwise noted the Soviet (Russian) version of events is related according to www.skywar.ru.
6 Naval History and Heritage Command https://www.history.navy.mil.
7 Details of the US version of the engagement according to *Flight Journal*, June 2013.
8 e.g. Voyenno-Istoricheskiy Zhurnal 2016 №12, Orlov, *Taynaya bitva sverkhderzhav* and others.
9 *Poteri VVS SSSR v Koreye* www.airwar.ru.
10 Mir Aviatsii №2(10)'95.
11 https://nvo.ng.ru/history/2017-03-24/1_941_poisk.html.

Chapter 7

1 Peterson, *Maybe You Had To Be There.*
2 Unless stated otherwise, this chapter is based upon Grisell, *The DC-3.*
3 Having stated that only one item was recovered it should be noted for the record that an unspecified "yellow object" which may have come from the DC-3 was also found washed up on the shores of Huvudskär island.
4 www.skywar.ru.

Chapter 8

1 Peebles, *Shadow Flights.*
2 Mir Aviatsii №1(24)2001.
3 Boyne, *Reconnaissance on the Wing.*
4 See Dabrowski, *Tsar Bomba.*
5 Pocock, *Operation 'Robin' and the British Overflight of Kapustin Yar.*
6 Pocock, *Operation 'Robin' and the British Overflight of Kapustin Yar.*
7 Orlov, *Taynaya bitva sverkhderzhav.*
8 Orlov, *Vozdushnaya razvedka SSHA nad territoriyey SSSR v 1950-1955 gg.*
9 An American U-2 overflew the site in September 1957 *Accomplishments of the U-2 Program* TCS-7519-60.
10 http://ncap.org.uk.
11 Brookes, *RAF Canberra units of the Cold War.*
12 Mir Aviatsii №1(24)2001.
13 Brookes, *RAF Canberra units of the Cold War.*
14 Mir Aviatsii №1(24)2001.
15 www.spyflight.co.uk.
16 Orlov, *Vozdushnaya razvedka SSHA nad territoriyey SSSR v 1950-1955 gg.*
17 Mir Aviatsii №1(24)2001.
18 Napier, *The Royal Air Force: A Centenary of Operations.*
19 All details (incl. quotes) of the story from the US side according to Austin's 307th Bomb Wing Association Newsletter No 30. Other sources may differ on particular details or quotes but do not negate the essence of Captain Austin's narrative.
20 Mir Aviatsii №1(24)2001.
21 Mir Aviatsii №1(24)2001.
22 www.airwar.ru.

Chapter 9

1 Peterson, *Maybe You Had To Be There.*
2 docs.historyrussia.org.
3 Mir Aviatsii №1(24)2001.
4 Peterson, *Maybe You Had To Be There.*
5 Krasnaya Zvezda 23 April 2008.
6 While observing the anniversary of an event having ostensibly taken place in October during November might seem like a bad Soviet joke, it in fact stems from the difference between the Old Style (Julian) and New Style (Gregorian) calendars.
7 Van Hare *Reds Down U.S. Bomber; 1 Dead* available at http://fly.historicwings.com.
8 Seydov, *91 Strategicheskaya Razvedyvatelnaya Eskadrilya v Koreye.*
9 Montgomery et al., *One Step from the White House.*
10 Peterson, *Maybe You Had To Be There.*
11 U.S.– Russia Joint Commission on POWs/MIAs.
12 *Aviatsiya i Kosmonavtika* 2011-10.
13 *Mir Aviatsii* 2001 01.
14 US Navy Patrol Squadrons https://www.vpnavy.org.
15 Peterson, *Maybe You Had To Be There.*
16 U.S.– Russia Joint Commission on POWs/MIAs.
17 www.skywar.ru.
18 Tayfun No 12 / 2012.
19 As a sidenote, more aircraft wrecks were found on Lysyy Ded's slopes: there was an Il-28 of the 1535 MTAP which went missing on 15 February 1955 with the loss of the entire crew, as well as a MiG-17 which crashed there in 1957, but in the latter case the pilot ejected, saving his life. https://dv.land/spec/aviapoisk.

Chapter 10

1 Public Papers of the Presidents of the United States: Dwight D. Eisenhower (1955) available at www.govinfo.gov.
2 For more details see Dabrowski, *Tsar Bomba*, pp.39–45.
3 The fact that General LeMay not only had nothing against unlashing a full-scale nuclear war against the Soviets but even on several occasions actively advocated such a move to US political leadership is attested by numerous sources such as, for example, Kaplan's *The Wizards of Armageddon.* It is to the great credit of the US presidents of those times, that they were not swayed by visons of a relatively easy victory in a nuclear war. One can only hope that the current and future generations of not just American but also leaders of all nuclear-armed states will show similar restraint.
4 Brown, *Dropshot: The United States Plan for War with the Soviet Union in 1957.*
5 Khrushchev held the posts of First Secretary of the Communist Party and that of the Prime Minister (Premier) of the Soviet Union being de facto and de jure the country's leader.
6 Orlov, *Taynaya bitva sverkhderzhav.*
7 Boyne, *Early overflights.*
8 The Department of State Bulletin Vol. 36.
9 Washington was the British designation for the American B-29 Superfortress in RAF service. Apart from their primary bomber role the aircraft were also utilised for electronic intelligence-gathering. *Canberra in the RAF.*
10 For more details see Dabrowski, *Hunt for the U-2*, pp.8.

11 Unless noted otherwise, U-2 missions, related details etc. are according to Pedlow et al., *The Central Intelligence Agency and Overhead Reconnaissance: The U-2 and OXCART Programs.*
12 Mir Aviatsii №1(28)2002.
13 Mir Aviatsii №1(28)2002.
14 Dokuchaev, 'Okhota v Stratosfere'.
15 Mir Aviatsii №1(28)2002.
16 Dokuchaev, 'Okhota v Stratosfere'.
17 Mir Aviatsii №1(28)2002.
18 Dokuchaev, 'Okhota v Stratosfere'.
19 US Department of State Bulletin, 30 July 1956.
20 www.onr.navy.mil.
21 Stratopedia http://stratocat.com.ar/stratopedia.
22 Mir Aviatsii №1(24)2001.
23 Mir Aviatsii №1(11)96.
24 Mir Aviatsii №1(24)2001.
25 Mir Aviatsii №1(11)96.
26 Stratopedia http://stratocat.com.ar/stratopedia.
27 Certainly not all the balloons the Soviets sighted were Genetrix ones; probably not a few were not spy blimps but genuine weather or other research aerostats.
28 Mir Aviatsii №1(28)2002.
29 Mir Aviatsii №1(24)2001.
30 www.encyclopedia.mil.ru.
31 Stratopedia http://stratocat.com.ar/stratopedia.
32 Pedlow et al., *The Central Intelligence Agency and Overhead Reconnaissance: The U-2 and OXCART Programs*
33 Mir Aviatsii №1(28)2002.
34 Pedlow et al., *The Central Intelligence Agency and Overhead Reconnaissance: The U-2 and OXCART Programs*
35 Mir Aviatsii №1(28)2002.
36 Dwight D. Eisenhower Presidential Library https://www.eisenhowerlibrary.gov.

Chapter 11

1 The list of incidents according to Winkler, *Cold War at Sea.*
2 Mir Aviatsii №1(28)2002.
3 Mir Aviatsii №1(24)2001.
4 Mir Aviatsii №1(24)2001.
5 The Department of State Bulletin Vol. 40.
6 Unless otherwise noted the Soviet version of events is related according to Orlov, *Taynaya bitva sverkhderzhav* but for a caveat: according to Orlov, the intercepting Soviet fighters were Yak-25s but he must be mistaken as all other sources such as, for example, Voyennyy Akademicheskiy Zhurnal 2016 No. 2(10), easternorbat.com and others maintain that fighter units of the Baku AD district were at that time equipped with MiG-17s.
7 Both Major Shupe as well as Colonel Brannon confirmed this with the caveat that the latter, while acknowledging that documents containing 'awful important information' were aboard, linked them not with the U-2 programme but with other highly sensitive intelligence operations. U.S.NEWS & WORLD REPORT, MARCH 15, 1993.
8 104-10124-10040 SUBJECT: American C-118 Aircraft Downed in Soviet Azerbaijan 27 June 1958 by Soviet MiG-17's available at www.archives.gov.
9 104-10124-10040 SUBJECT: American C-118 Aircraft Downed in Soviet Azerbaijan 27 June 1958 by Soviet MiG-17's available at www.archives.gov.
10 Time Jul. 21, 1958.
11 104-10124-10040.
12 U.S.NEWS & WORLD REPORT, MARCH 15, 1993.
13 The version of events is related herein according to Istoriya Aviatsii 2004 02.
14 According to a number of sources including Orlov, *Taynaya bitva sverkhderzhav*, Senior Lieutenant Lopatkov was credited with the kill.
15 Sovetskaya Aviatsiya 19 / 20 September 1958.
16 DOCID: 3901038 available at www.nsa.gov.
17 Peterson, *Maybe You Had To Be There.*
18 Dates and other details according to THE COMMUNICATOR Vol V, No. 32, 26 August 1997.
19 Peterson, *Maybe You Had To Be There.*
20 State Department press release of 5 February 1959.
21 For example, *Intercepted Conversation Throws Doubts on Value of Any Statements by Reds*, Washington Post 6 February 1959.
22 U.S.– Russia Joint Commission on POWs/MIAs.
23 www.arlingtoncemetery.net.
24 By a strange twist of fate, the demise of the C-130 was witnessed from the ground by a young man named Martin Kakosian, who became a skilled sculptor and later emigrated to America (he passed away in 2016). Once circumstances allowed for it, he sculptured a memorial at the crash site in the form of a *khachkar*, a traditional Armenian memorial stele bearing a cross as well as additional motifs and inscriptions. Unfortunately, the *khachkar* fell over and broke but Mr Kakosian sculpted another monument, this time modern in style, which replaced it at the crash site, with a replica placed at the National Museum of the US Air Force, Wright-Patterson AFB. Yet another memorial to the crew of 60528, the centrepiece of which is a Hercules withdrawn from service, stands at Fort Meade, Maryland.

Chapter 12

1 Mir Aviatsii №1(28)2002.
2 Unless otherwise noted, U-2s mission described according to Pedlow et al., *The Central Intelligence Agency and Overhead Reconnaissance: The U-2 and OXCART Programs.*
3 West, *Historical Dictionary of Cold War Counterintelligence.*
4 Mir Aviatsii №1(28)2002.
5 Dokuchaev, 'Okhota v Stratosfere'.
6 Richelson, *When Secrets Crash*, www.airforcemag.com.
7 Pedlow et al., *The Central Intelligence Agency and Overhead Reconnaissance: The U-2 and OXCART Programs.*
8 Pedlow et al., *The Central Intelligence Agency and Overhead Reconnaissance: The U-2 and OXCART Programs.*
9 Mir Aviatsii №1(28)2002.
10 Khrushchev, *Khrushchev Remembers: The Last Testament.*
11 Dokuchaev, 'Okhota v Stratosfere'.

Chapter 13

1 Central Intelligence Agency Photographic Intelligence Brief B-1009-59.
2 Pedlow et al., *The Central Intelligence Agency and Overhead Reconnaissance: The U-2 and OXCART Programs.*
3 Pedlow et al., *The Central Intelligence Agency and Overhead Reconnaissance: The U-2 and OXCART Programs.*
4 Dokuchaev, 'Okhota v Stratosfere'.
5 Samoylov, *Zagadka pervomaya 1960 goda.*
6 Dokuchaev, 'Okhota v Stratosfere'.
7 Samoylov, *Zagadka pervomaya 1960 goda.*
8 Knutov, *Pauersa sbil mayor Voronov.*
9 Mir Aviatsii №2(29)2002. The time was also given as 0836 hours by Dokuchaev, 'Okhota v Stratosfere' but it appears to be a mistake considering the timing of events as reported by the majority of sources.

10 Mir Aviatsii №2(29)2002.
11 Pedlow et al., *The Central Intelligence Agency and Overhead Reconnaissance: The U-2 and OXCART Programs.*
12 Mir Aviatsii №2(29)2002.
13 Dokuchaev, 'Okhota v Stratosfere'.
14 Presently the wreckage is exhibited at the Central Armed Forces Museum in Moscow, with a number of small fragments donated to a few other museums. In the latter context, it is interesting to note that once the USSR was no more, Russia handed over some small fragments of the aircraft to the United States which can be seen at the National Cryptologic Museum in Fort George G. Meade, Maryland, www.nsa.gov/History/National-Cryptologic-Museum.
15 Mir Aviatsii №2(29)2002 and Dokuchaev, 'Okhota v Stratosfere'.
16 www.pamyat-naroda.su.
17 Pedlow et al., *The Central Intelligence Agency and Overhead Reconnaissance: The U-2 and OXCART Programs.*
18 Powers & Gentry, *Operation Overflight: The U-2 spy pilot tells his story for the first time.*
19 www.arlingtoncemetery.net.
20 This talisman inspired the title of the book *The Little Toy Dog* by William L. White, which related the fate of the aircraft and its crew.
21 Dokuchayev, *Samolot-razvedchik RB-47* available at www.zvezdaweekly.ru.
22 U.S.– Russia Joint Commission on POWs/MIAs.
23 White, *The Little Toy Dog.*
24 Dokuchayev, *Samolot-razvedchik RB-47* available at www.zvezdaweekly.ru.
25 Dokuchayev, *Samolot-razvedchik RB-47* available at www.zvezdaweekly.ru.
26 Pedlow et al., *The Central Intelligence Agency and Overhead Reconnaissance: The U-2 and OXCART Programs.*
27 Peterson, *Maybe You Had To Be There.*
28 Ruffner, *Corona: America's First Satellite Program.*

ABOUT THE AUTHOR

Krzysztof Dabrowski from Poland has a lifelong interest in the subject of military aviation and has written dozens of articles on a variety of related subjects for printed magazines and the ACIG.org/ ACIG.info, AeroHisto and The Boresight websites. His particular area of interest is air warfare during the Cold War, the aircraft involved, and the experiences of their crews. He has published a number of books on related topics.